Praise For *The Coastal Forager's Cookbook*

"Kort's approach to cooking—a blend of 'simplicity and experimentation'—is an approach that teaches us to work with ingredients rather that make the ingredients work for us."

—*SCOUT MAGAZINE*

"Kort's book is as much a resource guide as it is a cookbook . . . Home cooks and outdoor enthusiasts also likely will appreciate the book's division into seasons, highlighting the foraged goods at peak freshness."

—*425* MAGAZINE

"The multitalented outdoorsperson-culinary artist isn't just highly skilled and extremely knowledgeable . . . she also takes gorgeous photos."

—*STIR* MAGAZINE

"Chef Robin's exploration and study of the wild edibles of the Pacific Northwest has opened up a whole new grocery list of ingredients and flavors . . . Her thoughtful use of these ingredients create a modern spin on classic recipes taking very unique flavors and making them extremely approachable and delicious."

—CHEF ROBERT BELCHAM

"A chance to save some money on groceries, try new recipes or incorporate new ingredients into familiar ones. It's an invitation, above all, to go out, explore and experience all that nature gifts to us."

—CULINARY HISTORIANS OF CANADA

THE COASTAL FORAGER'S COOKBOOK

FEASTING WILD IN THE PACIFIC NORTHWEST

CHEF ROBIN KORT

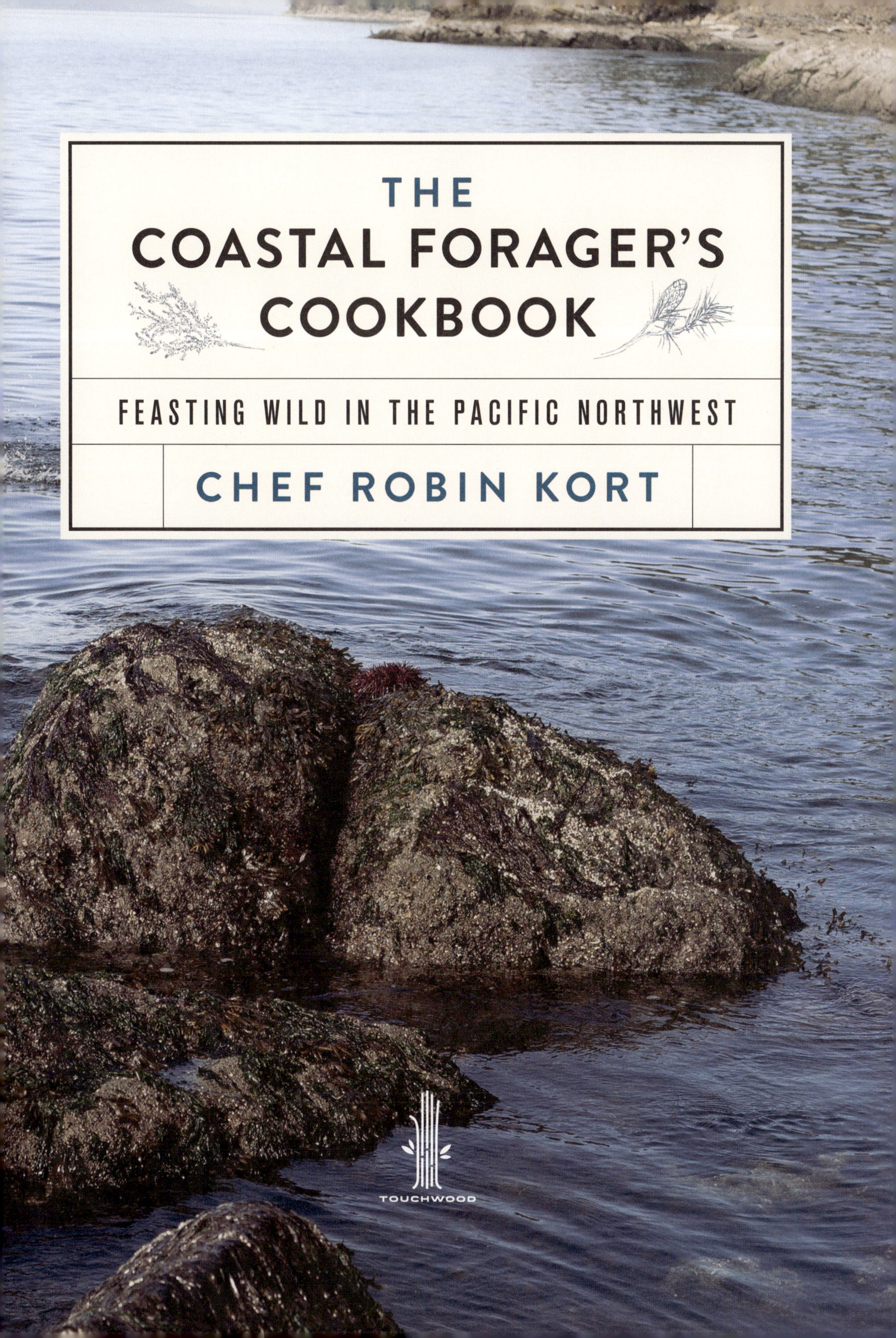

TOUCHWOOD

TouchWood Editions
touchwoodeditions.com

The information in this book is true and complete to the best of the author's knowledge. All recommendations are made without guarantee on the part of the author or the publisher. This cookbook describes traditional and contemporary edible wild plants, seafood, and fungi in the Pacific Northwest to help reconnect people with our wondrous natural world. Use of seafood, plants, or fungi as food should only be considered under guidance from an experienced wildcraft expert to help you with identification. A good rule of thumb is to spend at least a year to get to know any plant or fungi that you have an interest in consuming, allowing you time to gather as much information as possible about its habitat, poisonous relatives, and identification throughout the seasons. Plants and fungi can migrate to different regions over time, so it's also important to keep up to date on any new species they could be confused with. No wild plant, seafood, or fungi should be consumed unless you are absolutely certain of its identity and toxicity and of your personal potential for allergic reactions. The author (that's me, Robin) is not responsible for the actions of the reader.

Edited by Lesley Cameron
Cover and interior design by Lara Minja
Photography by Robin Kort, with the following exceptions: page 2–3, 91, 161 (Jimmy Allen); pages 6, 9, 11, 129, 136, 139, 167, 171 (Angela Fama); page 83 (Katie Dey); page 183 (Wikicommons, photo by EvelynL).
Illustrations by Heidi Sidhu

CATALOGUING DATA AVAILABLE
FROM LIBRARY AND ARCHIVES CANADA
ISBN 9781771514088 (hardcover)
ISBN 9781771514095 (electronic)

TouchWood Editions acknowledges that the land on which we live and work is within the traditional territories of the Lkwungen (Esquimalt and Songhees), Malahat, Pacheedaht, Scia'new, T'Sou-ke and W̱SÁNEĆ (Pauquachin, Tsartlip, Tsawout, Tseycum) peoples.

We acknowledge the financial support of the Government of Canada through the Canada Book Fund and of the Province of British Columbia through the Book Publishing Tax Credit.

This book was produced using FSC®-certified, acid-free papers, processed chlorine free, and printed with soya-based inks.

Printed in China

27 26 25 2 3 4 5

This cookbook is dedicated to all the curious cooks out there searching for a deeper connection to the forests and oceans of the Pacific coast through their food.

—ROBIN

CONTENTS

Introduction

I've spent a lifetime exploring the lands and waters of the Pacific Northwest with food in mind. My home is a paradise for foragers, and I've harvested more than a few pockets' worth of delicious plants, mushrooms, and seafoods throughout the years. Over this time, I've woven these wild ingredients into myriad recipes. Old family recipes passed down from my grandmother, chef friends, and mom keep me grounded and are the basis for all of my cooking. Cooking is like a form of meditation for me: repeating the same motions of cooks throughout time makes space for quiet contemplation and connection.

These recipes are a look into my life of traveling to places like Spain, Italy, and Japan to eat, cook, and learn from people and places with long traditions of using wild ingredients. At home, some of my dishes reflect the foraging expertise of Indigenous peoples who were living on the coast long before my family, and I am grateful for their help during my culinary journey through their lands and territories. This cookbook reflects my life as a coastal chef and strives to be a celebration of West Coast cuisine.

I am sharing my collected research with you in hopes that, like me, you will learn to connect the dots from wilderness to plate and begin to uncover some of the delicious secrets found everywhere in the Pacific Northwest, from the forest to the sea. My advice is to gently follow the seasons and harvest what is offered up fresh each month. In spring, we have the shoots and leaves; the flowers blossom and berries ripen in summer; we dig roots and gather fungi in the fall; and when winter's frost settles in and drives the mushrooms underground, we head to the sea to pluck mussels from the rocks. This is the seasonal dance, although the exact timing of the steps may vary. A careful eye will watch for when the maple blossoms sashay in and the elderflowers take the stage. Make a mental note of these subtle changes to guide your foraging for years to come. When flowers have lost their petals at lower elevations near the sea, follow the cooler air up into the mountains and, just like magic, you'll see that their sisters still have their blooms. Sometimes we lose touch with the natural rhythms of the seasons that are expressed by wild things. I believe it's important to relearn these patterns, remember the steps, and experience the joy in dancing with our plant-y partners. Nothing feels better than knowing how to move with the wilder world. I hope that you enjoy learning a few of my steps.

Happy foraging.
Chef Robin

Be a good forager

When I first learned to harvest seaweed, I fell in love with bullwhip kelp. As a child, I played with it on the beach. The long stem made a very good lash, which I used with gusto on my poor father. Later in life I encountered a long, wavy bouquet of shiny, brown ribbons slipping by my canoe in deep water on a paddling trip through Desolation Sound, at the northern end of the Salish Sea on the west coast of BC. I was so excited by my find! As the current pulled us past, I tugged on the bullwhip kelp and ripped it from its holdfast. A holdfast is the seaweed's root-like structure, which keeps it attached to the seafloor. As with any new wild edible find, I took the kelp home to feverishly research and recipe-test it. After consulting with experts, including some wonderful conversations with a local marine biologist named Amanda Swinimer, I learned that it's best to harvest healthy-looking detached or floating kelp rather than messing with active rooted kelp forests. Kelp forests are like nurseries for a multitude of sea life, so keeping them intact is essential. That information was very helpful, but it made me feel like I had stepped on a slug (sorry, little buddy!). So, what is the moral of the story? There is a good way to harvest each and every seaweed, wild plant, and sea creature. Please take the time to learn about how to honorably harvest before you pull, cut, or pick. Consider giving back to the wilds by cultivating native plants in your gardens or helping to keep abundant species in check by harvesting them responsibly. Nature deserves our respect, and that means taking a slow, considerate approach to what and how we harvest from the natural ecosystems that we all rely on. People can count on grocery stores, but birds, bees, and sea critters don't have that luxury. I don't harvest more than I can easily process and I never take more than 10 percent of what I find in abundance, with some exceptions—for example, an invasive (Himalayan blackberry) or overly productive species (like sea urchins). Remember to take the utmost care to pick only what is plentiful and leave the rest for other beasts. Okay, that's my rant, let's get cooking!

› Terms like weeds, plants, and herbs are somewhat interchangeable. More specifically, in this book, when I talk about herbs, I mean plants used as dominant flavorings like rosemary or evergreen tips. Edible weeds (though many are inedible and damaging to native ecosystems) can be seen today as pesky garden invaders, but the only thing that separates an edible weed from parsley or carrots is that modern humans have decided to cultivate one and not the other. For example, plantain (*Plantago* spp.) which is a leafy green not related to a banana, was historically used in food and medicine. Maybe it will come back into fashion as a cultivar in the near future.

Swallow Tail's test kitchen

Experimenting with new freshly harvested ingredients is the best part of my job. The kitchen of the Swallow Tail supper club in Vancouver, BC, is where all the fun happens. I bring baskets of mushrooms, net bags of seaweeds, and buckets of shellfish back from far-flung corners of the wilds of coastal British Columbia to play with. Black huckleberries, matsutake (pine) mushrooms, halibut, birch leaves, evergreen tips, and sea urchin are some of the tastes that I connect with my home. My "cuisine" is Pacific Northwest. My cooking techniques are influenced by Spanish, Japanese, Thai, and Italian methods. With that framework as a backdrop, here is my approach to creating a new recipe.

1. Find a wild ingredient that you're excited about (like porcini). Then research recipes that use that ingredient or integrate it into some of your own dishes.

2. Carefully assess the distinct characteristic(s) of the wild edible. Does the foraged ingredient taste similar to any other ingredient? For example, a fern root with a licorice aroma may make a good substitute for anise or fennel in a braise or marinade. What do you like about its taste, color, texture, or aroma that you want to highlight?

3. Use as few ingredients as possible. Always ask yourself if an ingredient highlights or masks the characteristics of the wild edible. Consider the strength of the hand-harvested ingredient and try to avoid adding any ingredients to the dish that will overshadow it. Some wild foods are gentle yet distinctive. For example, black huckleberries are lightly sweet and smoky, and their unique flavor would disappear in most cooked dishes. These berries might be better suited for a sorbet or simple cocktail or served fresh as the final accent on a simple base cake. In contrast, you might match a more powerful ingredient like Douglas-fir tips—which have musky rosemary notes—with a strong fish like salmon.

4. Keep all the tastes in mind—sweet, sour, bitter, umami, spice—when you start developing a recipe. The trick to making a successful new dish is to ring as many of these bells as possible.

5. Check for balance near the end of cooking. Sugar can be added as a last step to savory dishes and salt to sweet dishes if desired.

6. Finally, have fun experimenting. It's unlikely that you'll nail a recipe on your first shot. I tend to shoot from the hip with cooking, rarely using a recipe verbatim. Sometimes

I add ingredients seemingly at random (whatever needs to be used up in the fridge), which can result in either brilliance or disaster. Creating this cookbook enticed me to tame my wild mind and get everything down in black and white, so thank you. I hope you enjoy my experiments and taste the Pacific Northwest coast in every dish.

Unless otherwise specified in an ingredients list:

Butter is salted

Milk is full-fat (3.25%)

Heavy cream is 36%–40% fat

Whipping cream is 30%–36% fat

Pepper is freshly ground black pepper

Salt is sea salt or table salt

Sugar is granulated

Herbs and spices (including chili peppers and bay leaves) are fresh

Parsley type is your choice

Garlic is ideally organic or farm-grown (see page 85)

Fruits and vegetables that can be used peeled or unpeeled (for example, cucumbers) keep their peel

Wash vegetables and herbs and either pat herbs dry or use a salad spinner

SPRING

Spring: Shoots, leaves & edible trees

You can see where nature focuses her energy in the different seasons and follow through by picking a few of the edibles that are on offer. Spring is all about the bright green new growth of plants and is the start of my foraging season. Tiny leaves in early April are packed with flavor and the promise of a delicious dish. Bitter dandelion, sour sheep sorrel, fragrant elderflowers, peppery watercress, citrusy spruce tips and herbaceous birch leaves—there's something so energizing about these hopeful beginnings. Watercress soup with preserved winter truffle oil, dandelion marmalade on hot buttered toast, elderflower gin cocktails, fir tip vinaigrette on a wild green salad, morning birch tea—this is what spring tastes like to me.

My first harvest of the year is usually the magenta-colored blossoms of the flowering currant (*Ribes sanguineum*). This shrub can literally hum with bee activity. Flowering currant is a food hot spot for queen bumblebees as they emerge in the spring. Once I was buried in foliage harvesting and had a hummingbird hover right in front of my face, ignoring me completely while it fed. I nearly felt the breeze from its wings. I always forage respectfully, taking only a few clusters of flowers and treating them like a precious rarity rather than excitedly defrocking the whole bush. Be mindful of the hummingbird and insect pollinators that rely on the nectar of these first flowers. Even better, plant one or more native plants in your yard and nudge your city to plant more of them on boulevards. Their aroma is the perfect combination of sweet and savory; it will fill the streets with the scent of spring and inspire you to make delicious salads.

Later in spring, prince mushrooms (*Agaricus augustus*) are on my mind, so I keep a quiet eye on my usual spots as temperatures warm up and the rain comes. These savory fungi pop up from the forest duff and smell distinctively like marzipan (almonds). They look a bit like a huge portobello and have chocolate brown

gills when they're mature. When you press them or cut their stem, they bruise yellow, which is cool. As with all wild mushrooms, you have to be sure you know how to identify one correctly as there are many mushrooms with similar characteristics that could do harm to the careless. Apply this rule: "When in doubt throw it out." Or maybe just go with "Leave it be if unsure of ID." Think about taking a mushroom field trip with a local guide to learn more before you start picking.

There are way fewer edible mushrooms in spring than in fall, but if you're lucky, notable treats like chicken of the woods, wild oyster mushrooms, morels, and shaggy manes might present themselves to you. One of my favorites is the mysterious morel mushroom. I found some this year completely by chance under the drip line of our cabin, where we had been discarding wood shavings, making an accidental habitat for a fungal find. Morels love disturbed areas like this and form neat little lines of mushrooms here as well as at the edges of fire pits and forest fires.

STINGING NETTLE–STUFFED ZUCCHINI

Serves 6

3 large (each around 9 inches/ 20 cm long) zucchinis
1 cup (250 mL) stinging nettle leaves
3 Tbsp (45 mL) butter
¼ cup (60 mL) minced onion
1 large clove garlic, crushed
2 tsp (10 mL) sumac
Salt and pepper
½ cup (125 mL) crumbled (pea-sized pieces) feta cheese
¾ cup (180 mL) grated Gruyère cheese
3 Tbsp (45 mL) minced dill
1½ Tbsp (22 mL) all-purpose flour
3 eggs, beaten
Pinch of smoked Spanish paprika

Lime green nettles pepper the forest trails on Galiano Island, BC, for much of the year. In April, these stinging plants emerge to menace cyclists and hikers alike. What some of these people might not know is that the nasty leaves that sting their exposed ankles and arms can be quite beneficial. Nettle is as old as the hills, and many cultures across the world have made tea with nettle leaves to heal infections, reduce inflammation, or soothe sore muscles. I revere its earthy, rich flavor and tend to use it as a replacement for spinach in recipes.

Preheat the oven to 375°F and grease a rimmed baking sheet.

Slice the zucchini in half lengthwise. Scoop out the seed area with a spoon, making a trough, but leave a ¼-inch (1 cm) rim. Mince the zucchini scrapings.

Put on gloves to handle the fresh stinging nettles. Wash the nettles and discard the stems. (You can use them to make a tasty tea if you like.) Bunch the leaves into a ball and dice. In a frying pan over medium heat, cook the chopped zucchinis and nettles in the butter with the onions, garlic, sumac, and salt and pepper until soft, about 5 minutes.

Mix in the cheeses, dill, flour, eggs and salt and pepper to taste. Fill the zucchini cavities and dust with a pinch more sumac.

Bake on the prepared baking sheet until brown, about 30 minutes. Dust with smoked paprika and serve with roasted red peppers or a salad if you wish.

EVERGREEN CONE MOLASSES POPOVERS

Serves 4

EVERGREEN CONE MOLASSES

1 cup (250 mL) whole soft small green Scots pine cones (or green Douglas-fir cones)
1 cup (250 mL) packed brown sugar

POPOVERS

1 cup (250 mL) milk, divided
1 scant cup (240 mL) all-purpose flour (see Tip)
2 large eggs
½ tsp (2 mL) salt
¼ cup (60 mL) melted butter, for the pan

WHIPPED CREAM

1 cup (250 mL) whipping cream
3 Tbsp (45 mL) sugar

› A scant cup of flour is a loose cup, so it measures just slightly less than a full cup.

A few years back I read an article on mugolio, a traditional pine cone syrup from northern Italy. I thought to myself, "Hey, we have pine trees here too. Let's try this out." May rolled around and I walked my neighborhood doing a little "urban foraging" to look for Scots pine cones. The original recipe calls for new green cones, so I searched for dime-sized cones, picked some, and headed home to play. I found that this syrup is one of the easiest things you can make. All you need is sugar and fermentation time. There are endless possibilities with such a wild-tasting syrup: for example, drizzle it over blue cheese or add it to a whiskey sour. Please keep me posted on any of your own experiments.

(continued on page 28)

EVERGREEN CONE MOLASSES

Sterilize a 4-cup (1 L) mason jar.

Put the pine cones and sugar in the jar and stir to combine. Cover with a lid and place in a cool dark place to ferment for about 1 month. Open the jar once a week and stir the ingredients and taste it until you are happy with the flavor. After about two weeks, you'll see a liquid like molasses form in the jar. Once it's done fermenting, strain the molasses off and reserve it in a sealed jar.

POPOVERS

In a large bowl, mix 2 Tbsp (30 mL) of the milk into the flour to make a sloppy paste. This helps stop it from clumping. Beat the rest of the milk, the eggs, and the salt into the flour mixture until well combined. Cover the bowl with plastic wrap and let the batter rest for 1 hour on the counter.

Place a baking sheet on the bottom rack in your oven to reduce spillage as the popovers rise. Place a popover pan or a muffin tin in the oven and preheat the oven to 450°F. Melt the butter in the microwave or on the stovetop. When the oven reaches temperature, remove the hot pan.

Pour about 1 tsp (5 mL) of the melted butter into each cup. Divide the batter evenly between the cups and return the pan to the oven. Bake for 10 minutes. Reduce the oven temperature to 375°F and continue to bake until the popovers are golden brown, about 20 minutes. Use a knife to gently ease the popovers out of the tin and let cool slightly.

WHIPPED CREAM

Whip the cream and sugar until stiff peaks form, being careful not to overwhip. Cut a slit in the side of each popover, spoon in the whipped cream, and drizzle with pine cone molasses. Serve immediately.

MOREL STRATA

Serves 6–8

1½ cups (375 mL) minced onion
40 large fresh morels, cut in half, divided
6 Tbsp (90 mL) butter
1 cup (250 mL) cooked, strained, chopped spinach or young nettle leaves
2 Tbsp (30 mL) thyme leaves
1 Tbsp (15 mL) minced sage or flowering currant leaves
2 Tbsp (30 mL) lemon juice
8 cups (2 L) cubed (1-inch/2.5 cm cubes) crusty white loaf
2 cups (500 mL) grated fontina cheese
¼ cup (60 mL) grated Parmesan cheese
9 large eggs
2¾ cups (675 mL) milk
2 Tbsp (30 mL) Dijon mustard
¾ tsp (3 mL) salt
¾ tsp (3 mL) pepper
Pinch of ground cumin

Morels are fascinating fungi. They look like they come from outer space and can pop up in myriad interesting places. You'll find them growing by the hundreds in the charred black ash after a forest fire, scattered along forest trails or in your garden compost if you're lucky. They are great chameleons and likely to elude you until you find your patch. My family and I have had our share of fruitful and fruitless mushroom scouting trips. Every aspect has to be perfect, but given the right rainfall, temperature, and elevation, magic happens and you could be blessed with a bounty of morels. At their core, morels love disturbed areas, which humans create in spades.

In the kitchen, morels' honeycombed texture soaks up sauce. They are very meaty and are wonderful roasted with pork or chicken. Morels are a mushroom that must be cooked. Prepare this recipe for strata the night before you plan to bake it. The fresh thyme is essential and is a natural accent to the mushrooms. Thyme's sharp, almost floral notes are a perfect contrast to a morel's earthiness. If you really love your friends, serve the dish for brunch with bubbly, as it makes a perfect pairing.

Sauté the onions and half the morels in 3 Tbsp (45 mL) of the butter in a large, heavy skillet over medium-high heat until soft, about 5 minutes. Add the spinach, herbs, and lemon juice, and cook for about 3 minutes, just to reduce the amount of moisture, then turn off the heat.

Butter a deep 9- × 13-inch (27 × 33 cm) baking dish.

Spread one-third of the bread cubes in the prepared dish. Top with one-third of the morel mixture and one-third of each cheese. Repeat this layering with remaining bread, morel mixture, and cheese, so you have three layers of each.

(*continued on page 33*)

Whisk the eggs, milk, mustard, salt, and pepper together in a large bowl and pour evenly over the ingredients in the baking dish. Cover with plastic wrap and chill for at least 8 hours, or up to 24 hours.

The next day, let the strata stand at room temperature for 30 minutes while the oven preheats to 350°F.

Bake the strata, uncovered, in the center of the oven until puffed, golden brown, and cooked through, 50–60 minutes. Test for doneness by checking the center with a knife. If it's still wet, cook for another 5 or 10 minutes. Let stand for 5 minutes before serving.

Around the 40-minute point, place the remaining sliced morels in a large pan with the remaining 3 Tbsp (45 mL) of butter, the cumin and salt to taste. Cook on medium-high heat until brown, about 10 minutes. Add them to the strata as a topping.

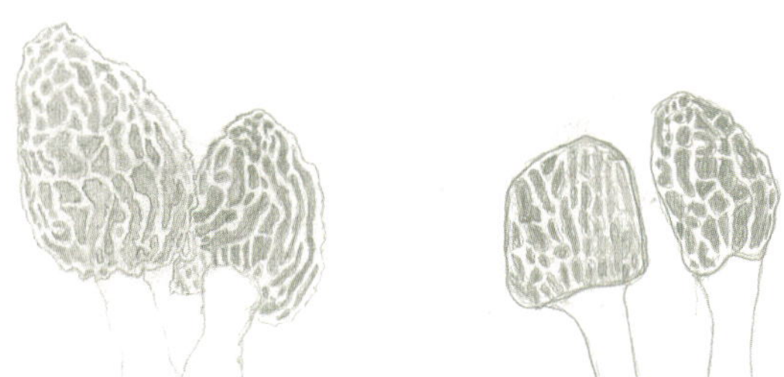

NETTLE PASTA WITH PECORINO

Serves 4

1 cup (250 mL) fresh nettle leaves or young shoots of Italian parsley
½ cup (125 mL) semolina flour
2 cups (500 mL) all-purpose flour
4 eggs
2 Tbsp (30 mL) olive oil
2 Tbsp (30 mL) butter
½ cup (125 mL) grated pecorino cheese
Cracked black pepper

› Pick only the new leaves of nettles for this recipe. Older leaves can be too tough to break down and so your pasta may not cut cleanly.

Nettles (*Urtica dioica*) have a delicious nutty flavor that really wows when you make pasta with them. I never pass up a chance to harvest a bag of nettles when I come across them, since the plant is such a prolific grower. Then I can make big batches of pasta and freeze it to use throughout the year.

Interestingly, not everyone is bothered by the acid compound that causes the sting of nettles, and some go so far as to eat nettles raw! If you fancy trying this, the trick is to crush the leaves thoroughly to break the tiny needles that deliver the sting. I am far too cautious to experiment with this party trick and instead always handle stinging nettles with gloves until they are cooked or dried, which neutralizes the sting. Pick them in spring when they are young and before they flower. If you cut the plant back, you'll get a second crop later in the year.

(continued on page 37)

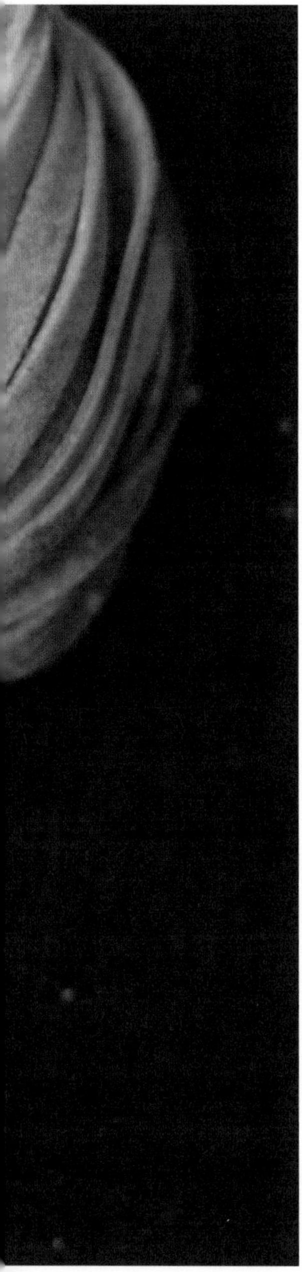

Place 4 cups (1 L) of cold water in a large bowl.

Boil a pot of water and salt it until it tastes like the sea. Add the fresh nettles and cook for 2 minutes. Remove them with a slotted spoon and place in the cold water for 10 minutes. Remove the nettles with tongs, fold them into a tea towel, and wring them out, then roughly chop them.

Put the nettles in a blender or food processor fitted with the steel blade, add both the flours, and mix until the nettles are very fine. Add the eggs one at a time, blending after each addition, and mix until it forms a rough ball.

Turn the dough out onto a floured work surface and knead until it becomes smooth, about 15 minutes, adding a little more flour if the dough is too sticky. Wrap in plastic and let rest for 20 minutes on your counter.

Break the dough into four sections, and rewrap three of them in the plastic. Form the dough into a flat square shape. Dust with flour and feed into a pasta machine, being sure to step through each thickness setting from 1 to 8. Cut the noodles tagliatelle size, 6 mm wide, either by hand or with your pasta machine. (If you don't have a pasta machine, you can hand-roll the pasta to 2 mm thick, dust well in flour, roll the dough loosely and cut into noodles.) Repeat with the three remaining pieces of dough, working with one piece at a time.

Bring a big pot of well-salted water to a boil over high heat. Add the fresh pasta and cook until al dente, 2–4 minutes depending on your preference. Toss in the oil and butter and serve with pecorino and pepper.

Portion out any uncooked pasta into four loose bundles, freeze them on a cookie sheet, and then put them in a sealed bag if you want to save the pasta to cook another day. You can cook it from frozen, but it will take a bit longer to cook.

WILD GREEN CANNELLONI (GF)

Serves 4
(Makes 8–10 cannelloni)

TOMATO SAUCE

1 large clove garlic, chopped fine
½ medium onion, chopped fine
2 Tbsp (30 mL) olive oil
1 handful lemon balm, diced fine (optional)
1 (28 oz/796mL) can whole tomatoes
2 Tbsp (30 mL) tomato paste
Salt and pepper

WILD GREEN SAUCE

¼ cup (60 mL) roasted pumpkin seeds
1 cup (250 mL) aromatic wild herbs (flowering currant leaf, miner's lettuce, sorrel, narrow leaf plantain, and lemon balm are all good)
2 Tbsp (30 mL) sliced leek, green part only
1 clove garlic
¼ cup (60 mL) olive oil
Salt

Narrow-leaved plantain, chickweed, dandelion, sorrel, and miner's lettuce are a few of the many abundant species of wild weeds in the Pacific Northwest that you can happily pluck to make into salads and green sauces. It's best to prepare this recipe in early spring, when the wild shoots of many plants like these are tender and packed with nutrients. The smaller, younger leaves are less bitter, so focus on picking those. Many wild plants get tough and tannic in later summer, though there are a few that stay juicy longer, like miner's lettuce, watercress, and sheep sorrel. I tend to harvest whatever looks tasty in my backyard; lemon balm and flowering currant leaves are especially wonderful. I encourage you to eat the weeds and try different aromatic wild herbs to make the green sauce in this recipe your own. Have fun!

TOMATO SAUCE

Sweat the garlic and onion in the oil for 5 minutes in a frying pan over medium heat. Add the lemon balm, tomatoes and their juice, and tomato paste and cook, stirring occasionally, until the sauce has a thick consistency. Add salt and pepper to taste. Let cool slightly, then blend in a food processor fitted with a steel blade until smooth.

WILD GREEN SAUCE

Purée all the ingredients until smooth in a food processor fitted with a steel blade.

(continued on page 41)

FILLING

2 cups (500 mL) full-fat ricotta cheese
1 large egg
½ cup (125 mL) grated Parmigiano-Reggiano cheese
Salt and pepper

VEGGIE "NOODLES"

1 large zucchini
1 large Japanese eggplant
Olive oil, for brushing

› Use good quality canned tomatoes for this recipe like Pomodoro Italian tomatoes. You really will taste the difference.

FILLING

Combine all the ingredients in a medium bowl. Add in the wild green sauce to this and mix.

VEGGIE "NOODLES"

Preheat the oven to 350°F. Grease a large baking sheet.

Using a mandolin, slice the zucchini and eggplant into long, very thin slices. Try to cut uniform, intact slices. These are your "noodles." Spread the slices evenly onto the prepared pan and sweat them in the oven for 15 minutes.

Assemble the cannelloni by laying down 2 slices of zucchini, overlapping slightly lengthwise, and 2 slices of eggplant overtop in the same manner like a spread of four cards. Put 3 heaping tablespoons (about 45 mL) of filling at one end of the layered vegetables and roll them up like large cannelloni. Continue in this way until you've used up as many veg slices as you can (some will be too small to use).

Spread about 1 cup (250 mL) of the tomato sauce evenly across the bottom of a 9- × 13-inch (23 × 33 cm) baking dish and then add the cannelloni in one layer. Brush lightly with oil and pour the remaining tomato sauce overtop.

The cooking time of around 45 minutes is variable and forgiving. Just bake in the oven at 375°F until the water has cooked off, the tomato sauce is saucy (not watery), and the cannelloni are browned. Let stand for 5 or 10 minutes before serving.

HALIBUT WITH FERMENTED BIRCH LEAF SAUCE (GF)

Serves 4

FERMENTED BIRCH LEAF SAUCE

1 cup (250 mL) young birch leaves (destem any older leaves)
2 limes, zested
1 large garlic clove, minced
½ tsp (2.5 mL) salt
½ cup (125 mL) lime juice (about 4 limes)
1 tsp (5 mL) fish sauce
1 cup (250 mL) minced napa cabbage
½ cup (125 mL) minced onion

HALIBUT

4 (each 8 oz/250 g) halibut fillets (about 1-inch/2.5 cm thick), skin on
Kosher salt
Grapeseed oil
1 cup (250 mL) young birch leaves, patted dry

As far as I'm concerned, halibut, which is a native Pacific flat fish, is the best-tasting fish, hands down. It's richer than cod, flaky and firm. One fish can weigh hundreds of pounds, so I tend to buy them whole from Steveston Fisherman's Wharf, in Richmond, BC, in May and fillet them into meal-sized portions to enjoy in the coming months. Bright green new paper birch leaves sprout around the same time. These leaves are tender and can be used much like green tea or as an herb to flavor dishes. Pour some boiling water over them and notice their fresh, slightly peppery aroma. They make a perfect complement to freshly caught halibut as a sauce. Think of them as similar to basil leaves.

FERMENTED BIRCH LEAF SAUCE

Put the birch leaves, lime zest, garlic, salt, lime juice, and fish sauce into a food processor and mince well. Transfer to a clean 4-cup (1 L) Mason jar and mix in the cabbage and onions. Drape a clean tea towel over the jar and leave to ferment for 3 days in a cool, dry cupboard.

Drizzle in enough oil to cover the green sauce, then secure a lid on the jar and refrigerate. To store for a longer period, place scoops of the sauce into an ice-cube tray and freeze them, transfer to a resealable freezer-proof bag, and use as needed.

FISH SKIN AND BIRCH LEAVES

You can ask your fishmonger to remove the skin for you so you don't have to do it yourself later. Take the fish and fish skin out of the fridge and let stand for 15 minutes. Line two baking trays with paper towel.

Cut the skin from the flesh of the fish with a sharp knife if it's still attached and pat dry. Slice the skin into ½-inch (1 cm) long pieces. Place ½ inch (1 cm) of the oil in a wide, deep pot or wok over medium

(*continued on page 44*)

heat and bring to 375°F. It should shimmer but not smoke. Fry the birch leaves until there are no bright green patches left, about 10 seconds, then remove to one of the prepared trays and dust with salt. Add the fish skin to the hot oil and cook until crispy, about 10 minutes. Remove to the remaining prepared tray to drain and then dust with salt.

HALIBUT

Preheat the oven to 170°F. Line a baking tray with paper towel.

Cut each fillet in half and pat dry. Season each side generously with salt. Keep the pot on medium and the oil at 375°F. Add each halibut fillet to the hot oil. Cook until golden brown, 4 minutes, then flip with tongs and cook for another 2–4 minutes, depending on fish thickness. Don't overcook them! Transfer to the prepared tray to remove some of the excess cooking oil and then place in the warm oven while you fry the remaining fish.

Serve each person 2 pieces of fish with a heaping tablespoon of sauce on the side. Top with crispy fish skin and fried birch leaves and a few fresh birch leaves for color.

› The key to success when you're frying anything is keeping the oil hot, especially as you put your ingredients into it. Using a candy thermometer to make sure the oil stays at the right temperature is the easiest way to do this, but in this recipe you can also fry each piece of fish separately to help maintain 375°F throughout cooking.

› A crisp white wine or rosé is a perfect pairing for this dish.

› You can also serve this as a stand-alone appetizer for 8 people by splitting each fillet in half before you fry it.

› Grapeseed oil is a good high-temperature, neutral-flavored oil for frying. You can also use peanut oil.

SABLEFISH WITH ORANGE, HAZELNUT, AND UNI SAUCE (GF)

Serves 4

SAUCE

2 Tbsp (30 mL) olive oil
1 medium onion, roughly chopped
2 celery ribs chopped
2 heaping Tbsp (35 mL) grated ginger
1 tsp (5 mL) salt
14 oz (395 g) sweet potato, roughly chopped
2 cups (500 mL) canned whole or crushed tomatoes
½ cup (125 mL) uni roe (or 2 Tbsp/ 30 mL anchovy paste)
1 medium orange, zested
3 cups (750 mL) water
2 cups (500 mL) chicken or vegetable broth
½ cup (125 mL) orange juice
½ cup (125 mL) hazelnuts

Sablefish is the kind of fish that melts in your mouth. It's also known as black cod or butterfish. (They changed the name for marketing reasons—"sablefish" sounds so much more expensive, doesn't it?) Its high fat content makes it a very forgiving fish to cook as it's hard to dry out from overcooking. Partner this silky white fish with a zesty citrus and added complexity from bitter hazelnuts and savory uni and I think we have a showstopper of a dish.

SAUCE

Warm the oil in a deep, heavy-bottomed pot over medium heat and sauté the onion, celery, ginger, and salt until transparent, about 5 minutes. Add the sweet potatoes, tomatoes (with their juice if you're using whole tomatoes), orange zest, water, broth, and orange juice. Bring to a boil and then turn down the heat to simmer until the sweet potato is tender. Let cool slightly.

Place the hazelnuts and uni roe in a blender with 1 cup (250 mL) of the warm sauce and blend on high speed until smooth. Add the rest of the sauce and blend until very smooth. Taste the sauce and re-balance with more orange juice for tartness, add more salt to taste, and cut with broth to thin if necessary.

(continued on page 49)

SABLEFISH

4 (each 8 oz/225 g) sablefish fillets (about 1-inch/ 2.5 cm thick), skin on
Kosher salt
Grapeseed oil (see page 44)

GARNISH

1 cup (250 mL) chopped watercress, escarole, or sorrel, or a mix of fresh wild bitter greens

SABLEFISH

Cut each fillet in half and pat dry. Season each side of the fillets generously with salt.

Add ½ inch (1 cm) of oil to a high-sided frying pan and heat on medium to 375°F. Cook the sablefish for 4 minutes until golden brown, then flip and cook for another 2–4 minutes, depending on fish thickness. Don't overcook them! You may have to cook them in batches to make sure that you don't overcrowd the pan which can reduce the cooking temperature and produce a less crispy result. Transfer to plate with a paper towel to remove some of the excess cooking oil.

Pour the sauce into four bowls, place 2 pieces of fish on top, and garnish with the watercress.

› This recipe also works well with halibut.

WATERCRESS TUNA TARTARE (GF)

Makes 40 canapés

6 oz (170 g) sashimi-grade tuna loin
¼ cup (60 mL) minced watercress, stems and leaves
2 Tbsp (30 mL) dandelion blossoms, torn into pieces
1 heaping Tbsp (20 mL) finely ground young lemon balm leaves
1 Tbsp (15 mL) chives, minced
1 tsp (5 mL) celery leaves, minced
1 Tbsp (15 mL) hazelnut oil
1 tsp (5 mL) lime juice
Salt and pepper
1 English cucumber, sliced into 40 (¼-inch/½ cm) rounds
1 Tbsp (15 mL) furikake (optional, page 78)

› You can use oregano instead of lemon balm, celery stalk instead of celery leaves, arugula instead of watercress, and radicchio instead of dandelion leaves.

The mustard family of plants can range widely in spiciness depending on the species, the age, and the time of year you harvest. Even watercress, which is part of this cohort, bought in the grocery store can be mildly to sharply peppery, so I recommend that you use your taste buds and alter this recipe according to your taste. I like to harvest bitter-cress in spring, because it grows abundantly in my backyard. Its seed pods pop when you touch them, spreading them everywhere. Use the flowers of wild mustard if you find any growing in your area. They're particularly beautiful in this dish.

Let the frozen tuna sit at room temperature for about 15 minutes, but don't let it thaw completely. It will cut more easily if it's still somewhat frozen.

Using a sharp knife, mince the frozen tuna. Transfer to a bowl and mix in the watercress, dandelion blossoms, lemon balm, chives, celery, oil, lime juice, salt, and pepper to taste.

Place a small spoonful of tartar on each cucumber slice, and dust with furikake (if using).

DANDELION MARMALADE (GF)

Makes 3 cups (750 mL)

- 2 cups (500 mL) finely chopped young dandelion greens (if your greens are extremely bitter then use more whole yellow flowers and fewer leaves)
- 2 cups (500 mL) finely chopped radicchio
- 2 cups (500 mL) sugar, divided
- 1 cup (250 mL) butter, divided
- 2 cups (500 mL) orange juice
- 1 cup (250 mL) balsamic vinegar
- 1 orange, zested
- 1 bay leaf
- 1 tsp (5 mL) thyme leaves
- 4 whole cloves, crushed
- ½ tsp (2.5 mL) ground cinnamon
- 4 juniper berries, crushed

Dandelion is often vilified as a garden weed that we chuck in the compost. However, if you believe in the tenets of Italian cooking, you might want to reconsider this approach, because bitter is where it's at. Bitter is an important component of the taste rainbow. In fact, the more parts of your tongue you can light up, the more interesting your food will be—think radicchio or coffee. Don't be afraid of bitter. It can improve digestion and add zip (like a chili) to any salad or dish. The level of bitterness in dandelion depends on when you harvest it and which part of the plant you eat. In early spring, the new leaves are fresh and only slightly bitter and the flowers aren't bitter at all. At my supper club, dandelion marmalade was one of my most popular recipes. Its taste is sweet, salty, sour, and bitter, which makes it an all-around winner. Serve with duck for dinner or on buttered toast in the morning.

Place the dandelion greens and radicchio in a medium saucepan over medium heat with 1 tsp (5 mL) of the sugar and ½ cup (125 mL) of the butter. Allow everything to caramelize, stirring occasionally, about 5 minutes. Add the remaining sugar, the orange juice, balsamic, orange zest, bay leaf, thyme, cloves, and cinnamon.

Reduce the liquid over medium-high heat, stirring constantly and keeping an eye on it so that it doesn't burn, until quite thick, about 30 minutes. Once it is jammy, add the rest of the butter, turn down the heat to medium and, stirring occasionally, let it thicken nicely, about 10–15 minutes. Now taste. Every wild ingredient has a natural variability, so you may have to add more sugar if your greens were very bitter. Mix in the juniper at the end.

Store in an airtight container in the fridge. Heat it slightly before using if you are going to use it as a sauce.

(continued on page 57)

› This goes particularly well with grilled duck breast.

Preheat your grill to 400°F. (You can use a charcoal grill or propane barbecue.) Score the fat of the duck breast (one breast per person) in a tight cross-hatch pattern, taking care to cut only fat, not meat. Salt and pepper the meat well on both sides. Place the duck skin-side down on the barbecue and cook for 3 minutes. Use a spray bottle with water to control any flare-ups. Flip the duck and cook for about 1 minute. Test the meat by pressing it (it should be soft but spring back quickly; you have to cook a lot of duck to get the feel for this) or more easily by using an instant-read thermometer. A perfect medium-rare is 130°F. Let the duck rest for 3 minutes. The temperature should go up to 135°F. Serve over buttery mashed potatoes and steamed asparagus and top with dandelion marmalade.

FLOWERING CURRANT RICE PUDDING (GF)

Serves 4

2½ cups (625 mL) water
½ tsp (2 mL) salt
1 cup (250 mL) arborio rice
5 cups (1.25 L) milk
⅔ cup (160 mL) golden raisins
½ cup (125 mL) sugar
2 Tbsp (30 mL) butter
¼ tsp (1 mL) vanilla extract
¼ cup (60 mL) minced
currant leaves
Flowering currant blossoms
and leaves, for garnish

My mom craved desserts, so I grew up licking batter spoons and measuring ingredients at her side. I loved making sweet treats like savarin cake and crêpes. I'd take them to school as a way to make new friends. Pouring over Mom's old cookbooks was soothing to me. I'd bake treats from them for when Dad came home from work. Sweetly spiced rice pudding was a special family favorite, and as I got older and my experiments with wild ingredients picked up steam, I played with flavoring it with currant blossoms. The flowers' pungent sage-like aroma seemed a natural replacement for the usual cinnamon.

(*continued on page 60*)

Bring the water and salt to a boil in a heavy-bottomed pot over high heat, then add the rice, cover and bring down to simmer for 15 minutes. (You can also use 3 cups/750 mL cooked rice and skip this step if you prefer.)

Add the milk, raisins, and sugar to the pot, and stir to combine. Bring back up to a boil over high heat, then turn down the heat and simmer, uncovered, stirring occasionally, until the pudding thickens slightly, about 20 minutes. At this point it will still look soupy. It will thicken more as it cools, so make sure to not overcook, as it may curdle. Stir in the butter, vanilla, and minced currant leaves and remove the pot from the heat. Serve hot or cold, according to your preference, with currant blossoms and leaves for garnish.

› "Fresh is best" is my rule for using flowering currant, because the flowers don't dry very well.

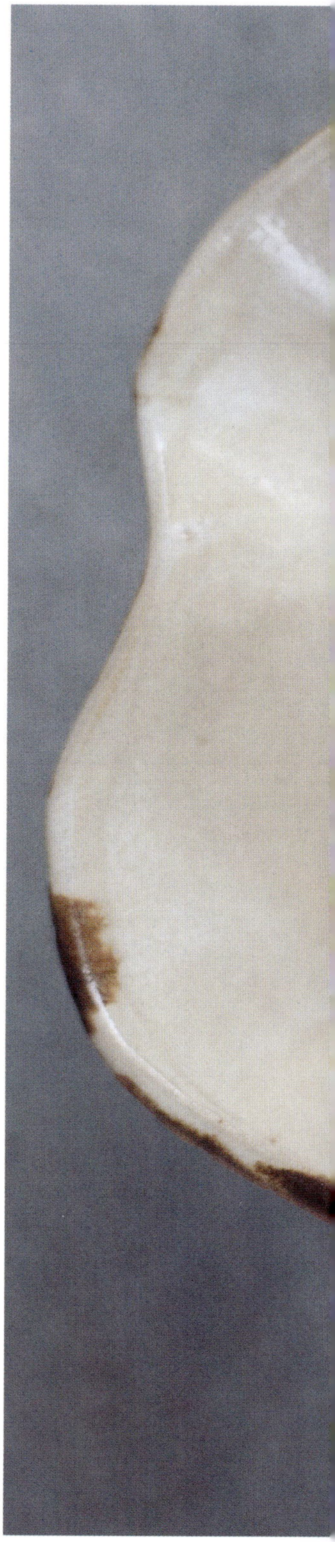

TANGERINE LEMON BALM CAMPARI ICE (GF)

Makes 2 cups/500 mL of ice

1 medium-sized tangerine
⅓ cup (80 mL) sugar
1 heaping tsp (8 mL) minced dill
1 heaping tsp (8 mL) finely chopped lemon balm or mint
1 tsp (5 mL) Campari
2 cups (500 mL) ice cubes

Lemon balm is one of the most vivacious plants in my garden. The birds spread the seeds everywhere, giving lemon balm the reputation of being an annoying weed. The term "weed" sounds so menacing, though. I prefer to think of these vigorous non-native plants as very akin to humans in their earthly success. Humans spread seeds, just like birds, carrying their food and medicine with them either knowingly or not. I like to encourage people to eat their edible weeds. Ancient plants like dandelion and lemon balm were once such important medicinal plants that travelers brought them across continents. With that in mind, let's use them in our kitchens again.

You can serve this as a cocktail with a shot of amaretto, or as an adult dessert. I love to swirl it with a scoop of vanilla ice cream. It tastes like a Creamsicle, which conjures happy childhood memories for me.

Zest the tangerine and put the zest in a blender. De-seed the tangerine segments and add them to the blender. Add the sugar, dill, lemon balm, and Campari and purée until smooth.

Wrap the ice in a clean tea towel and hit it with a hammer to loosely break it up. This is the key to getting a good consistency—you can't have large chunks of ice. Add to the blender and pulse until the mixture is like a sorbet (or a slush) in texture, 30 seconds to 1 minute. Do not blend too long or you'll have soup instead of an ice. Put it in an airtight plastic 4-cup (1 L) jar and freeze, or spoon it into an ice-cube tray if you want neatly portioned palate cleansers to serve to fancy people.

EVERGREEN ICE CREAM (GF)

Makes 4 cups (1 L)

1 cup (250 mL) milk
½ cup (125 mL) destemmed evergreen tips, divided
4 egg yolks
½ cup (125 mL) sugar
1 cup (250 mL) heavy cream, chilled

When spring arrives, I replace the rosemary in my pantry with fresh conifer tips from evergreen trees like Sitka spruce, true fir (*Abies* spp.), and Douglas-fir. Pick the young, green growth as soon as it emerges from the tip of each stem. I only pick tips from mature trees, as little trees are just starting out and I wouldn't want to inhibit their growth. If you ask me, evergreen needles should be a pantry staple in the Pacific Northwest, just as native oregano is in parts of Italy. Conifer needles have different aromatic nuances depending on the species, but broadly taste of citrus with bright, foresty notes. They have a completely unique taste: imagine crisp winds over lofty mountain tops. They can be used as a pot herb, sprinkled over salmon, simmered into sauces, or infused into sweets like ice cream.

(*continued on page 69*)

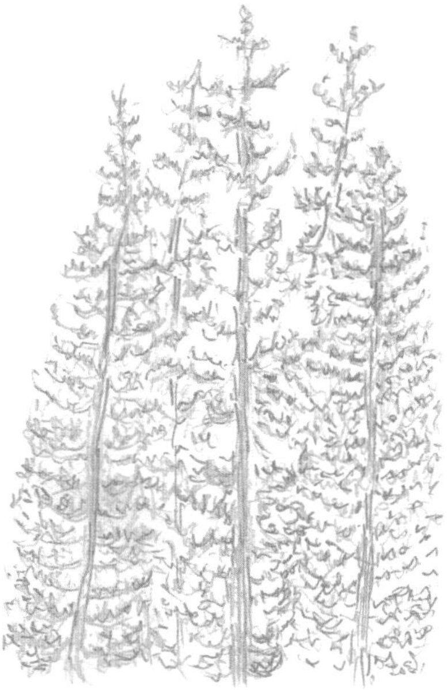

Pour the milk into a saucepan over medium heat. Bring it slowly up to boiling point, watching to make sure it doesn't boil over, and then turn off the heat. Place ¼ cup (60 mL) of the evergreen tips in the pan and leave to infuse for 20 minutes.

In a bowl, beat together the egg yolks and sugar. Carefully remove the tips from the milk and gently squeeze any residual liquid from them back into the pan. Stirring constantly, pour the hot milk into the egg mixture. This is called tempering and it helps keep your sauce from curdling. Pour the milk and eggs back into the pan and heat gently on medium, stirring constantly, until the custard thickens, about 5–10 minutes. Do not let it boil or it will curdle. When you can see a creamy film form over the back of your spoon, it's time to remove the saucepan from the heat.

Stir in the cold cream, mince the remaining conifer tips, and then add them to the cream mixture. Leave to cool, uncovered, at room temperature. Transfer the whole mixture into an ice cream maker and freeze according to the manufacturer's instructions.

› You can use this as a custard sauce if you don't have an ice cream maker. Pour it over poached fruit or cake

› It's best to use new spring needle growth rather than old. If you use older, tougher needles, blend the final custard till smooth.

ELDERFLOWER POACHED PEARS (GF)

Makes 2 × 4-cup (1 L) Mason jars

2 cups (500 mL) sugar
2 cups (500 mL) water
2 cups (500 mL) elderberry blossoms
5 ripe pears
6 long, wide strips of lemon rind, free of pith, divided
¼ cup (60 mL) lemon juice (about 3 large lemons)
1 tsp (5 mL) whole peppercorns, divided

The collected traditional plant knowledge of the Indigenous coastal peoples is invaluable to my cooking. Case in point, in the Pacific Northwest, many Indigenous peoples eat cooked berries or flowers of the elderberry plant, knowing that other parts can be harmful and understand that it's best not to eat the berries raw. Without this knowledge, my own first harvest years ago wouldn't have been advisable. There are more than twenty different species of elderberry (*Sambucus* spp.) across the globe, some more edible than others. In Europe, *Sambucus nigra* is historically used in traditional cooking whereas in North America, *S.cerulea*, among others, are more frequently used. Along the coast, the blue elderberry is traditionally cooked into a jam or juiced, strained, or used to marinate salmon.

Sterilize a 4-cup (1 L) Mason jar.

Make a simple syrup by placing the sugar and water in a medium pot over high heat. Bring to a boil and then keep at a boil for around 10 minutes, stirring occasionally, until the sugar dissolves.

Pack the elderflowers into the jar and pour the hot simple syrup overtop leaving 1 inch (2.5 cm) of space at the top. Screw on the lid, let cool, and then set the jar in the fridge for a week, shaking every 2 days. Remove from the fridge, strain the contents through a sieve set over a large bowl, and discard the flowers and any solids. Voilà, you now have elderflower syrup.

(*continued on page 72*)

Sterilize two 4-cup (1 L) Mason jars.

Pour the elderflower syrup into a pot and bring to a boil over medium heat. Slice the pears in half, core them, and divide them between the two jars with the lemon rind, lemon juice, and peppercorns. Pour in enough hot syrup to cover the pears, leaving about ¼ inch (1 cm) of space at the top, and secure the lids on the jars. Let cool on the counter (the lids will seal as this happens), then refrigerate. These should last for at least 2 weeks in the fridge, even after opening.

> I love slicing the poached pears and serving them on baked puff pastry with a dollop of mascarpone.

> This recipe can also be canned for longer preservation; search online for simple instructions on how to preserve fruit in syrup. You can store any extra elderflower syrup in the fridge. It's amazing in cocktails, sodas, or used for making desserts like sorbet.

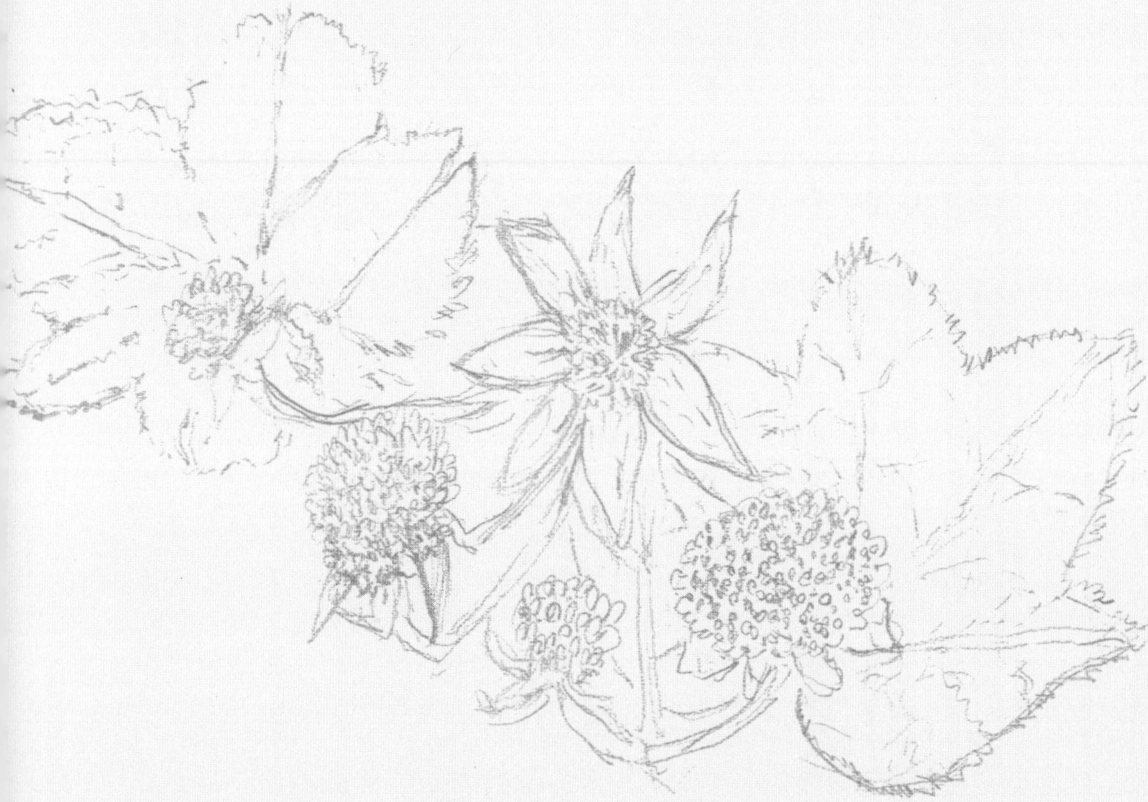

SUMMER

A lifetime of summer harvesting

My favorite place to hide out at age ten was high in a huge tree in the middle of Stanley Park, in Vancouver, BC. My parents would take me to the park and leave me to climb that old cedar for hours. I'd gleefully scale the limbs to the highest reaches and hang upside down by my knees off a perfect U-shaped branch. This skill translated well to fruit-picking, which was the start of my hunter-gatherer passion. The bigger the fruit tree, the more fun I had. Summer picking was a Kort tradition. Led by my grandparents, the whole family (some grumbling and some in their element) would be drawn out to harvest peaches, apples, plums, saskatoons, and blueberries. There are eaters and pickers, and my mom was decidedly an eater, so her bucket was always nearly empty. We'd bring the ripe fruit home to my grandmother's kitchen, where we'd make pickled plums, freezer jams, and saskatoon berry pies. Canning happened over idle chat with little dessert snacks like cinnamon-spiced fruit pastry twists and butter tarts. Cooking and eating together was an integral part of our family bonding ritual, which is probably true in many a home. Even family members who weren't naturally drawn to each other were lured into enjoying each other's company over strong coffee, sweets, and old stories.

On a more contemplative note, through a lifetime of summers on the Pacific Northwest coast, I've seen the new century bring about a shift in our local climate and weather patterns. It's become hot and dry for long, worrying stretches. There are years when the osoberries turn to raisins on the bush. Meanwhile, coastal cedars are literally falling over because of drought, and recent shellfish die-offs in the heat of what is now called fire season have been shocking. I don't remember smoke from wildfires in the Interior region of BC ever invading the coast while I was a kid, but now it's a regular occurrence.

Take the time to observe the subtle and not so subtle changes around you. Over time, if you go back to a harvest location again and again, you'll notice when a pattern changes—sometimes for the better and sometimes for the worse. Foraging makes you more aware of your effect on the world because you watch it with more attention to detail. I don't harvest much in the tough, smoky summers when the wildlife is struggling. Harvest in summer with care in your heart.

I hope you find some love in the fruitful summer recipes in this chapter to connect you to the earth and strengthen ties with the ones you love.

BULLWHIP KELP–FURIKAKE SPICE MIX (GF)

Makes 1½ cups (375 mL)

½ cup (125 mL) bullwhip blades, roasted and crumbled fine
½ tsp (2.5 mL) ground green peppercorn (Sichuan)
½ cup (125 mL) toasted white sesame seeds

Growing up in Vancouver, I naturally had a craving for the simple perfection that is Japanese cuisine. I have since traveled to Tokyo to cook and learn some of Japan's culinary techniques, including how to cook with and preserve seaweeds. Seaweed is an algae and is an essential component of any Pacific coastal pantry. Bullwhip kelp is an umami-rich seaweed that can be easily identified and sustainably harvested. I developed this recipe as a local nod to that addictive Japanese spice mix, furikake. Sprinkle it on rice, salads, or fish. It is at once salty, spicy, and nutty-tasting.

Bullwhip blades are like kelp leaves. They grow in the subtidal zone, so I wade out into cold clear water at very low tides, and cut about 30 percent off the blades with a knife, leaving lots intact so the kelp continues to live. The more you wash the blades the less salty the mixture will be. I don't rinse mine if they aren't muddy or sandy. I love salt!

Mix together all the ingredients and transfer to an airtight container. Store at room temperature for up to 1 year.

› Cooking the bullwhip blades until crisp over charcoal or a fire imparts the best flavor, but you can also bake them in a 375°F oven until they snap like a cracker, 10–15 minutes, depending on the size of each blade.

BULLWHIP GINGER PICKLES (GF)

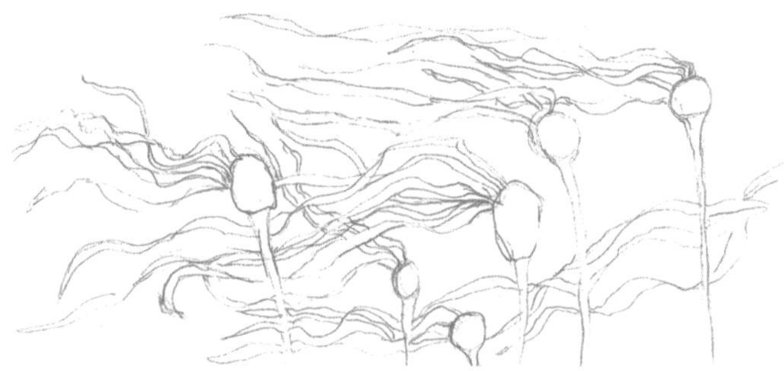

Makes 4 cups (1 L)

1 large bullwhip kelp stem (stem 2 inches/5 cm wide at the thickest part) or 2 smaller ones
¾ cup (180 mL) apple cider vinegar
2 Tbsp (30 mL) rosemary leaves
3 slices (about ½ × 1 inch/ 1 × 2 cm) of ginger
2 large cloves garlic
2½ Tbsp (37.5 mL) fish sauce

One sunny summer day, when I was standing on the dock on Galiano Island, BC, I plucked a floating bullwhip from the sea. "Bullwhip pickle is an old coastal recipe made as a sweet pickle," said my neighbor Steve, who was tinkering with his boat nearby. It got me thinking, but I really don't like sweet pickles, so I made a savory recipe instead that evening and loved it. I like to serve the pretty rings on charcuterie plates with salmon gravlax, chopped into a potato salad, or served with flame-grilled rich fish like skate, salmon, or sablefish.

You can eat the stem, float, and blade of bullwhip kelp. Only harvest healthy-looking stems that you find free-floating on the ocean—never pull them up from their holdfast on the ocean floor. Be careful not to harm the kelp's capacity to regrow, as it provides ample habitat for other sea creatures.

(continued on page 85)

Sterilize a 4-cup (1 L) Mason jar.

Cut the bullwhip stem into 1 mm rounds and pack them tightly into the prepared jar, leaving 1 inch (2.5 cm) of space at the top.

Place the apple cider vinegar in a small pot with the rosemary, ginger, garlic, and fish sauce and bring to a boil over medium heat. Adjust the strength of the pickling liquid by adding water to taste. Pour the hot mixture over the bullwhip slices and watch them turn bright green with heat. I like crunchy pickles, but if you want a softer texture, put the bullwhip in with the vinegar to boil for 20 seconds.

Cover the jar with plastic wrap (which stops the metal lid from reacting with the vinegar) and screw the lid on. Allow to cool, then put the pickles in the fridge to store (they should last for 6 months at least) or serve them right away.

› I recommend using organic garlic for cooking. It's usually much stronger in flavor, so even though it's more expensive, you use less in recipes and so you're actually ahead of the game.

› If you harvest older, larger bullwhip in fall, its stem will be tough, so peel it before pickling.

SEA ASPARAGUS GAZPACHO

Serves 4

½ cup (125 mL) sunflower oil
4 large garlic cloves, minced very fine
30 (each 3 inches/7.5 cm long) shoots of sea asparagus, divided
2 cups (500 mL) vegetable stock (or dashi, page 186)
¼ cup (60 mL) amontillado (or your favorite medium sherry)
¼ cup (60 mL) balsamic vinegar
16 oz (450 g) filleted sockeye salmon, cut into 1-inch (2.5 cm) cubes
6 oz (170 g) scallops or shrimp
¾ tsp (3 mL) ground cumin
2 Tbsp (30 mL) thyme leaves
⅓ cup (80 mL) + 2 Tbsp (30 mL) olive oil
1 tsp (5 mL) smoked paprika
⅓ baguette (4 oz/100 g) sliced thin
4 large pieces crostini (or toast) per serving

Sea asparagus has a satisfying, salty, grassy taste similar to a green bean, which is why they are also called sea beans. Folks tend to pickle or fry them or eat them raw. Raw is best, in my mind, as it preserves their crunchy texture. I love to add them as a briny, zippy addition to any dish. Sea asparagus carpet salt marshes and turn slowly from green to red in late summer. They are best hand-picked in early summer when they are still olive green, but can be harvested later in the year as well, though they get tougher and more bitter with time.

For a vegetarian option, top this dish with cooked sweet corn instead of seafood.

Heat the sunflower oil in a small, deep saucepan over medium heat until shimmering but not smoking. Add the garlic, spread it evenly across the pan, and remove from the heat as soon as it starts browning, about 1 minute. Be careful not to over-brown it, as it will turn bitter. Transfer immediately to a metal bowl to cool. Brush the sea asparagus with the garlic oil from the pan (you won't need all of it) and chop half the shoots into 1½-inch (3 cm) pieces, setting aside a few for garnish.

Bring the stock, sherry and balsamic to a boil in a frying pan over medium-high heat, then turn down the heat to a simmer. Add the salmon, scallops, cumin, and thyme and cook until they turn opaque, 2–4 minutes. Be careful not to overcook them. Remove the seafood with slotted spoon to a large bowl and add the 2 Tbsp (30 mL) olive oil, paprika, and 1 Tbsp (15 mL) of the fried garlic, toss it and salt to taste.

In another large bowl, pour the hot stock over the bread slices to soak for about 30 minutes.

(continued on page 88)

6 ripe medium tomatoes
½ green bell pepper, cored and deseeded
½ red bell pepper, cored and deseeded
6 Persian cucumbers (or 1 English cucumber)
1 small red onion
1 small serrano chili, deseeded
1 lime, quartered

Decide how spicy you want to make your gazpacho and use less chili if desired. Rough chop all the vegetables, dust with salt, and let sit for 20 minutes. Blend them in a food processor until smooth, then add the soaked bread, and all the juices. Process until the mixture is smooth and then, with the machine running on high speed, slowly drizzle in the ⅓ cup (80 mL) of olive oil and another 1 Tbsp (15 mL) of the fried garlic. (If you add it too quickly, your soup may break.)

Serve in bowls and top with crostini, a handful of the cooked seafood, and the sea asparagus shoots, then dust with a touch more smoked paprika and more fried garlic. Serve with lime wedges.

› Keep the leftover fried garlic to add to other recipes that use garlic. You can also buy pre-cooked fried garlic at some Asian grocery stores; I usually have some in my pantry at the ready for lazy days.

SEA LETTUCE BREAD STICKS

Makes about 40 sticks

1½ cups (375 mL) bread flour
½ cup (125 mL) kamut flour (or whole wheat flour)
1 tsp (5 mL) instant yeast
¾ tsp (4 mL) salt
¼ cup (60 mL) sea lettuce or nori, diced fine, tossed with 1 tsp (5 mL) all-purpose flour
⅞ cup (205 mL) warm water
1 Tbsp (15 mL) olive oil, plus more for brushing
Cracked salt, for sprinkling

Sea lettuce can be found along the west coast from Alaska to California and is best harvested in early summer. Find the translucent, wide blades and snip them from the rocks, then rinse them in clean sea water and dry in the sun, or bake at 150°F for about 20 minutes or until they are cracker-crisp to preserve them. Sea lettuce, also called green laver, has the "greenest" flavor of all the kelps. The taste is very bright and similar to asparagus. Referred to as aosa in Japanese cuisine, sea lettuce is used as a flavoring for traditional omelets and in sauces and as a finishing herb. It will keep its luscious green color even when cooked. I love using it as a topping for risotto.

Mix together all the ingredients except the cracked salt and then knead until smooth, 5 minutes. Cover the bowl with a damp tea towel or plastic wrap and let the dough rise in a warm, draft-free spot until it has doubled in size, about 2 hours, depending on how warm your room is.

Preheat the oven to 350°F. Grease a baking tray.

(*continued on page 93*)

Roll the dough into a ½- × 6-inch (1 × 15 cm) rectangle on a lightly floured counter. It will be about ¼-inch (0.5 cm) thick. Cut into long, ¼-inch (0.5 cm) wide strips. Twist and stretch each strip of dough into the shape of a breadstick. They should be no more than ½-inch (1 cm) thick at any point. Place them on the greased baking tray, brush them lightly with olive oil, and sprinkle with cracked salt.

Bake until cracker-crisp and nicely browned, 25–35 minutes. Serve with butter or uni butter (page 134).

CUMIN-CRUSTED SURF SMELT (GF)

Serves 4 as an appetizer

3 Tbsp (45 mL) whole cumin seeds
3 Tbsp (45 mL) hazelnut flour (or all-purpose flour)
2 tsp (10 mL) salt
1 tsp (5 mL) pepper
16 surf smelt fish
4 tsp (20 mL) peanut oil (or grapeseed oil)
2 limes, sliced in half

I lived in Barcelona for a spring and ate fresh sardines grilled on an open fire there. So simple, so good. When I returned home, I searched for something similar to this salty treat, but all our local fish seemed to be big, like ling cod, salmon, and halibut, so it took me a while to find an alternative. At Spanish Banks in Vancouver, I had seen people fishing from the shore for surf smelt in mid-August when the fish run in the waves. The fishers patiently cast their gillnets and wade out to catch these little tasty fish. That summer, I finally spotted surf smelt in a local market and took some home to fry. Happily, they turned out to be very like the fresh sardines from my memory with a lean white flesh and delicate crunchy bones that you can eat with the meat.

Toast the cumin seeds in a frying pan over medium heat until it turns brown. Remove from the heat and grind them with a mortar and pestle or in a spice grinder. Combine the cumin with the flour, salt, and pepper.

Pat the fish dry with a paper towel, then press each fish into the flour mixture.

(*continued on page 96*)

Preheat the oven to 170°F. Line a baking tray with paper towel.

Heat the oil in a frying pan over medium-high heat until it shimmers but doesn't smoke. Fry the fish 4 at a time for about 2½ minutes on each side until they're brown and crispy. (The cooking time will depend on the thickness of the fish.) Place them on the baking tray and keep warm in the oven as you cook each round, or serve them to guests hot as you finish cooking them. Serve with a half of lime on the side, and eat the whole fish, head to tail.

› If you can't find surf smelt, try using another fresh small fish like sardines.

ALDER-SMOKED SALMON BELLY (GF)

Makes as much as you have fish

6 lb (2.7 kg) salmon belly (chinook or steelhead is ideal)
Kosher salt
1 round 6- × 6-inch (15 × 15 cm) piece of alder wood chopped into kindling or equivalent amount of alder catkins, or kindling of other good smoking wood like maple or apple
1 bag hardwood charcoal

Red alder catkins are great for adding delicate, sweet smoky flavors to your food and they are very sustainable, as you can just gather them as they fall off the tree. Soak them in water, bundle them up in a little aluminum foil, and poke holes in the package to infuse food with smoke on a gas grill or use them in a smoker if you can't find bigger chunks of alderwood. Ask your fishmonger if they have any large salmon belly pieces—they usually will, if not you can buy whole salmon and cut the belly pieces from the fish. Serve this with a nice green salad and rice.

Brine the salmon belly in a plastic or glass container by dissolving kosher salt in cold water until it tastes salty enough to suit your palate (for me, that's when it tastes like the sea). Make sure the fish is covered completely and refrigerate it overnight. Remove it from the water and pat dry with a tea towel. Develop the pellicle by leaving the fish to air dry for 1–4 hours in a cool place on a grate (under 59°F), under a fan, or at a breezy window. This forms a shiny coat for the smoke to adhere to. Don't skip this part, it's essential! The salt will protect the fish from going off, so don't worry about that.

(*continued on page 101*)

To smoke the fish, place it on an oiled grate in the smoker to the side of wherever you are starting the fire. I have an offset firebox in my smoker which keeps the fish from overcooking. Start the fire with hardwood charcoal and then add your smoking wood to that. Keep your smoker at about 225°F for about 1 hour or until the salmon fat is rendered. The timing will vary depending on its thickness.

If you don't have a smoker, use a gas or charcoal barbecue. To barbecue the salmon belly, place it to the side of the open fire. This simulates an offset smoker, but will cook the fish faster (never put the fish over the flame). Belly is very forgiving, so overcooking won't be a problem. Cook, skin-side down, until the fat has rendered, about 20 minutes. This is a great campfire option for the recipe.

› You can also use sockeye salmon belly, but if you do, cook it for less time as it tends to be leaner. You can also use this recipe to smoke fillets or other fish cuts. Just vary the smoking time based on how fatty your fish is—it works like a charm.

SPOT PRAWNS WITH BEAKED HAZELNUT SAUCE

Serves 4 as an appetizer

HAZELNUT DIPPING SAUCE

- 2 tsp (10 mL) coriander seeds, toasted
- ½ tsp (2.5 mL) cumin seeds, toasted
- Pinch of ground cinnamon
- 1 large lemongrass stalk minced, white part only
- 3–5 dried red Thai chilies (depending on how spicy you like it), toasted
- ½ cup (125 mL) roasted hazelnuts
- 1 (14 oz/410 mL) can coconut milk
- 2 large garlic cloves, minced
- ¼ cup (60 mL) minced onion
- 2 Tbsp (30 mL) brown sugar
- 2 tsp (10 mL) minced cilantro stems
- 1 tsp (5 mL) minced ginger or galangal
- 1 tsp (5 mL) shrimp paste (or uni roe, page 134)
- 2 Tbsp (30 mL) fish sauce
- 7 Tbsp (105 mL) chopped preserved lemons (page 106) or lemon juice

Beaked hazelnuts are a beautiful native nut shrub. You can harvest the nuts as long as the squirrels leave a few for you in late summer or early fall. You can watch them turn brown and harvest them in fall or harvest them green a bit earlier. My biologist friend Ficus Chan introduced me to picking them green rather than waiting until they dry out. You have to pick them at the perfect time: too early and they are very tannic and bitter, but late enough in the summer they are a juicy and lightly sweet nut. I've spotted my neighborhood squirrel, whom I call Doug, testing young hazelnuts by biting into them and tossing them away if he deems them unripe. I guess that's squirrel composting!

HAZELNUT DIPPING SAUCE

Finely grind all the dried spices, lemongrass, and chilies with a mortar and pestle or spice grinder, and set aside. Grind the nuts in a food processor and then add the ground spices.

Pour the top two-thirds of the coconut milk (the thicker stuff) into a saucepan, add the garlic and onions, bring to a boil over medium-high heat, then turn down the heat to low and simmer for 10 minutes. Add the ground spices and chilies and cook for 5 minutes, then add the rest of the ingredients except the lemons. Taste and balance with fish sauce and brown sugar to your liking. Cook for 5 more minutes, just until you see that the sauce has thickened. Stir in the lemons at the end to keep it sharp-tasting.

(*continued on page 104*)

PRAWN FRY

1 cup (250 mL) toasted panko
½ cup (125 mL) finely grated Parmesan
1 lemon, zested
1 egg, beaten
1 lb (500 g) prawns, shelled, tails left on
½ tsp (2.5 mL) salt
2 cups (500 mL) peanut oil
Roasted popweed (page 162), seaweed, or steamed asparagus, to garnish (optional)

PRAWN FRY

Mix the panko with the Parmesan and lemon zest. Dip each prawn in egg, then panko mixture, sprinkle with salt, and set aside.

Add in the oil to a high-sided saucepan so that it's about 1 inch (2.5 cm) deep and warm over medium-high heat until it just shimmers. It should be 375°F. Deep-fry the prawns in batches for 30 seconds a side, bringing the oil back to temperature after each batch. Never overcrowd the pan. Drain the fried prawns on paper towel and serve them with the dipping sauce and (optional) garnishes.

› If you can't track down beaked hazelnuts, regular will work just fine.

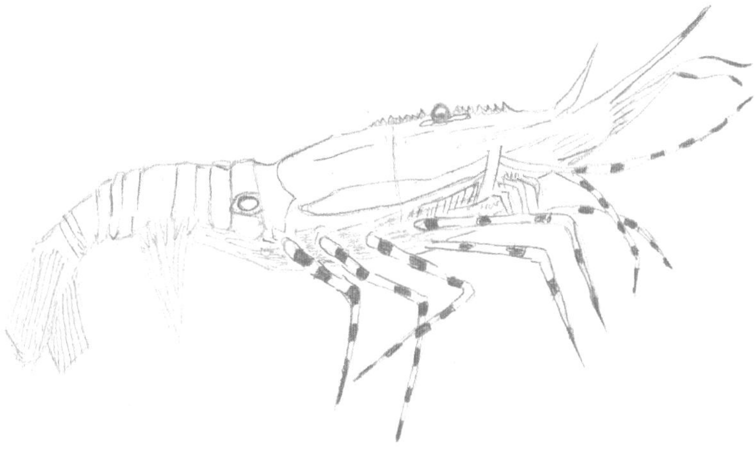

PRESERVED LEMON AND SEAWEED-WRAPPED SALMON (GF)

Appetizer for 4

PRESERVED LEMONS

10 organic lemons (Meyer are best), divided
Kosher salt

MARINADE

1 Tbsp (15 mL) brown sugar
1½ tsp (1 mL) mustard powder
½ tsp (2 mL) pepper
1 tsp (5 mL) grated ginger
½ cup (125 mL) water
½ cup (125 mL) soy sauce
¼ cup (60 mL) sake
2 Tbsp (30 mL) hazelnut oil

Wild chinook, pink, and sockeye salmon are all gorgeous Pacific salmon that each have a special place in my kitchen. Pink is great canned and sockeye, always so lean, is perfect flash-frozen for sashimi. Chinook (king) salmon is my choice for smoking, baking, or grilling. It has a good amount of fat and is rich, flaky, and flavorful. I don't tend to buy farmed salmon, as the meat of so-called Atlantic salmon is too soft and mild for my tastes unless I'm making a pâté. There are also a lot of questions around the environmental impact of salmon farms, although some are working hard to counteract this. The main reason you may want to eat farmed fish is the price, so if you must, stick to land-locked farms to avoid impacting the health of wild salmon territory. (Note that you need to make the preserved lemons 3 days before you plan to eat this dish. You can also find them in Iranian grocery stores premade, if you want to use store-bought.)

PRESERVED LEMONS

Using a mandolin or sharp knife, slice 5 of the lemons as thin as you can, removing any seeds. Layer 3 slices in a 4-cup (1 L) Mason jar, sprinkle ½ tsp (2.5 mL) kosher salt over top, and repeat with the remaining lemon slices.

Juice the remaining 5 lemons and pour the juice over the lemon slices to cover them. Cover the jar loosely with a cloth and let sit on the counter for 3–5 days to ferment, taste it to see if you want to ferment further, then seal and refrigerate. These will keep and mature in flavor for up to 6 months (even once opened) in the fridge.

MARINADE

Mix together all the marinade ingredients.

(continued on page 109)

SALMON PACKETS

24 oz (680 g) king salmon fillet, skin and pin bones removed, sliced into 3-inch (8 cm) square pieces, about 1-inch (2.5 cm) thick

Salt

2 cups (500 mL) peanut oil, for frying + extra for brushing

4 (each 8 × 8 inch/20 × 20 cm) store-bought sheets of nori seaweed (see Tip if you want to use foraged)

FOR SERVING

2 cups (500 mL) cooked rice

4 slices preserved lemon, for garnish

2 Tbsp (30 mL) fried garlic, for garnish

2 Tbsp (30 mL) grated ginger, for garnish

1 tsp (5 mL) toasted sesame seeds, for garnish

SALMON PACKETS

Remove the skin from the salmon and marinate the salmon for at least 3 hours, or up to overnight, in a non-reactive container in the fridge. Make sure the salmon is fully immersed in the marinade.

Meanwhile, cut the salmon skin into 1-inch (2.5 cm) squares. Place the peanut oil in a small deep pot and bring to 375°F over high heat. Fry the salmon skin pieces until crisp, about 1 minute, then transfer to a paper towel and dust with salt. You'll use these to crumble over the final dish.

Preheat the oven to 450°F. Lightly grease a rimmed baking tray.

Remove the salmon from the marinade and pat dry.

The seaweed will naturally stick to the damp salmon, but brush it with a little water to make it fold easily. Place each salmon piece on top of a seaweed sheet and lightly brush the fish with peanut oil. Tuck and fold it into a neat package. Place seam-side down on the prepared baking sheet, and bake for 6–8 minutes, depending on fillet thickness, or until an internal temperature of 125°F is reached.

To serve, slice each package in half and place on top of the rice. Top with a slice of preserved lemon and some fried garlic, ginger, and sesame seeds, and then crumble some of the fried salmon skin over it all.

› If you want to use foraged nori rather than store-bought, use three large (similar-sized) sheets, overlapped, for each wrap.

› Flat seaweed blades of all kinds can be used in this recipe. Use one large piece of winged kelp blade with the stem removed in place of the nori sheets, or three large sheets per wrap, overlapped, of sea lettuce, fresh black or red nori.

› I like to serve this with Japanese rice, but your favorite long-grain rice would also work well.

THIMBLEBERRY JAM AND SCONES

Makes 3 (1-cup/250 mL) jars of jam and 22 scones

JAM

2 cups (500 mL) ripe thimbleberries
3 cups (750 mL) sugar
1 oz/25g pectin powder (I like Certo)
Pinch of salt
Pinch of ground juniper berries (optional)

SCONES

1¾ cups (415 mL) all-purpose flour
¼ cup (60 mL) hazelnut flour
4 tsp (20 mL) baking powder
½ tsp (2.5 mL) cream of tartar
½ tsp (2.5 mL) salt
½ cup (125 mL) cold butter
1 cup (250 mL) ice-cold buttermilk (or whole milk)
1 egg, beaten, for brushing
Cracked salt, for sprinkling

At my grandmother's breakfast table, you'd find a bounty of fruit preserves—most likely apricot, peach, or cherry—and her homemade bread with a rainbow of summer jams. She taught me by example that you should cook along with the seasons to yield the most delicious results.

My gift to you is my favorite jam recipe. This recipe is for small-batch refrigerator jam, so there's no need to can it, as it gets eaten pretty quickly. Thimbleberry jam tastes like a really intense raspberry jam, but sweeter and more concentrated. Thimbleberries are very delicate, so don't worry if they end up squished, as you'll be making jam anyway. The downy leaves of the bushes often conceal the summer berries from casual passersby, leaving lots for you to discover if you take the time to look under a leaf.

(continued on page 112)

JAM

Mix the berries, sugar, and pectin in a small, deep pot and bring to a boil over medium-high heat, stirring continuously. Stir on high heat until the jam thickens, about 5 minutes. If you are not sure if the jam is thick enough to set, take a small spoonful and put it in the freezer to cool. This will let you check the consistency to make sure it's gelled. Once cooked, mix in the salt and juniper berries and pour into clean jars, screw the caps on tightly, and cool to seal, then refrigerate. Keeps for approximately 2 weeks in the fridge and 3 months in the freezer once opened.

SCONES

Preheat the oven to 450°F. Grease a baking sheet.

Place both flours, the baking powder, cream of tartar, and salt in a food processor fitted with the steel blade. Mix to combine. Break the butter into four chunks, add to the dry ingredients, and pulse until the butter pieces are pea-sized. With the machine running on slow, pour in the buttermilk in a slow stream. Only add enough for all the dry flour to disappear and the mixture to clump together (you may not need all the milk), and try not to overmix.

Handling the dough as little as possible, form it into a ball, put in a plastic bag, and place in the freezer for 15 minutes to chill.

Dust the counter with flour and turn the dough out onto it. Roll it to ¾-inch (2 cm) thickness and cut out rounds with a 2-inch (5 cm) pastry or cookie cutter (or use the floured rim of a glass). Brush the tops with the beaten egg and a pinch of cracked salt. Transfer to a greased baking sheet and cook all the way through, about 7–9 minutes. If in doubt, tear a piece off a scone and check it's cooked before removing them from the oven.

› There are so many unique-tasting berries on the Pacific Northwest coast. Try making salmonberry, salal berry, osoberry, Oregon grape, black huckleberry, or wild blueberry jam. These will all need more sugar than thimbleberry jam depending on how sweet you like it. You can always add more sugar until you like the taste and then reduce the jam by cooking it down until it's the thickness you like.

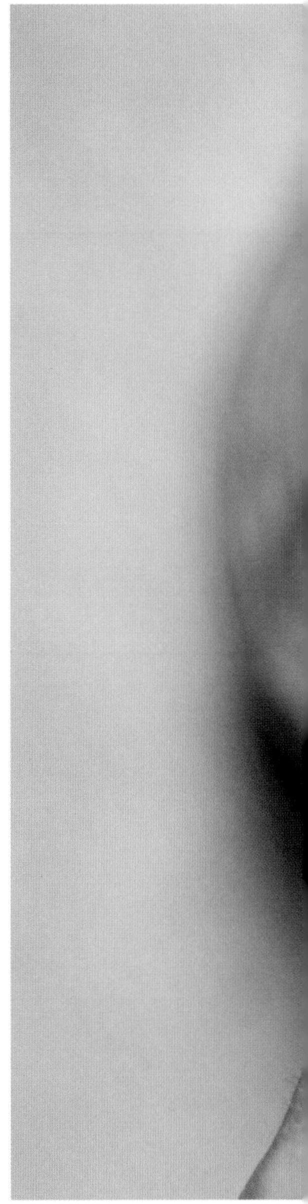

BLACK HUCKLEBERRY CAKE (GF)

Makes 1 (9-inch/23 cm) cake

CAKE

2 Tbsp (30 mL) shredded unsweetened coconut
5 large egg whites
9 oz (250 g) sugar
7 oz (200 g) almond or hazelnut flour
1 tsp (5 mL) lemon zest
¼ tsp (1 mL) white pepper

CUSTARD

5 large egg yolks
3½ oz (100 g) sugar
½ cup + 2 Tbsp (150 ml) whipping cream
3½ oz (100 g) cubed butter
2 tsp (10 mL) vanilla extract or elderflower syrup

TOPPING

2 cups (500 mL) fresh red or blue huckleberries or blueberries
½ cup crushed roasted walnuts

Huckleberries have an alluring sweet-tart flavor with delicate, oaky notes. You may find them snuggled in among wild blueberries. The two bushes are very similar and belong to the same genus, *Vaccinium*. Huckleberries are an important traditional food for many Indigenous peoples along the west coast of Canada and the USA. The berries can be cooked into a fruit leather or mixed with salmon roe for a savory dish.

In the kitchen, try adding huckleberries to salads, fish dishes, or sweets like trifle, muffins, or compotes. You can also substitute the more tart red huckleberries in this recipe. I tried this cake for the first time at a friend's wedding and tweaked it to feature wild berries. It is sweet and decadent and is the perfect base to show off any wild summer berries.

CAKE

Preheat the oven to 390°F. Heavily butter a 9-inch (23 cm) spring form pan, and sprinkle the bottom and sides with the coconut.

Beat the egg whites into stiff peaks on high speed. Turn down the speed, then slowly add the sugar until gooey peaks form, about 2 minutes. Gently fold in the almond flour, lemon zest, and pepper, and then pour the batter into the cake pan.

Bake until the cake is just set, 20–25 minutes. The center should be firm and browned. Let the cake cool.

(continued on page 117)

CUSTARD

Whisk together the egg yolks, sugar, and cream in a saucepan over medium heat. Stir continuously until the sauce has thickened, about 5 minutes. Mix in the butter and vanilla. Transfer to a bowl, cover tightly with plastic wrap, and chill fully in the fridge to set.

TOPPING

When the cake and custard are both cool, top the cake with the custard, fresh berries, and walnuts—and you are done!

> This cake turns out best when you measure your ingredients super accurately. For best results, use the measurements listed in grams.

PINEAPPLE WEED AND WILD BLUEBERRY PANNA COTTA (GF)

Serves 8

1 large handful of pineapple weed, about 20 stems with blossoms (3 inch/7cm tall), divided
1 cup (250 mL) milk
2¾ tsp (14 mL) gelatin
2 cups (250 mL) blueberries
3 cups (750 mL) heavy cream
6 Tbsp (90 mL) sugar
Pinch of salt

When I'm teaching my field students about this aromatic plant, I tell them to crush a tiny yellow blossom between their fingers and notice the distinctive fruity scent of pineapple. Sometimes your nose is the best aid to identifying wild edibles.

Pineapple weed (*Matricaria discoidea*) is an urbanite. I spy it stubbornly upright on hard-packed dirt trails in the heat of early summer. It blossoms just as many wild berries ripen, which makes them a natural pair for experimentation in my kitchen. Panna cotta is a dessert that highlights subtle flavors like wild coastal berries, so I've been making this recipe at my supper club for many summers. Try it with salmonberry, blueberry, or black huckleberry for a lightly sweet cooling treat.

Set aside 8 flowering buds of the handful of pineapple weed for a garnish.

Place half of the pineapple weed in a small pot with the milk, bring to a boil over medium heat, then simmer for 10 minutes. Remove from the heat and leave to cool fully. Remove the pineapple weed, squeeze out any excess milk, and discard the cooked pineapple weed. Top up the milk to make 1 cup (250 mL). Pour the milk into a clean saucepan, sprinkle the surface with the gelatin, and let soak for 10 minutes.

Put eight (approximately 8 oz/235 mL) serving glasses on a baking sheet and add a handful of blueberries to each one.

Make an ice bath by filling a large bowl with 4 cups (1 L) cold water and 2 cups (500 mL) ice. Place a smaller bowl in the bath and add the cream and the remaining raw pineapple weed chopped fine.

Reheat the milk on high, stirring continuously, for about 1½ minutes. Remove from the heat and stir in the sugar and salt until dissolved, 1 minute. Pour the milk into the cream, stirring until it thickens to the consistency of eggnog or test it with a candy thermometer (it should be 50°F), about 10 minutes. Divide the mixture evenly between the serving glasses. Cover the glass tightly with plastic wrap and let the panna cotta set for at least 4 hours, and up to 3 days, in the fridge.

Garnish with 1 blossom of pineapple weed per cup and serve.

OREGON GRAPE GIN COCKTAIL (GF)

Makes 4 drinks

OREGON GRAPE SIMPLE SYRUP
Oregon grape juice
Sugar

ALCOHOLIC COCKTAIL
4 oz gin
1 oz Oregon grape simple syrup
8 oz tonic water
Ice to fill four lowball glasses
2–3 sage leaves per glass for garnish

NON-ALCOHOLIC COCKTAIL
3 oz Oregon grape simple syrup
12 oz soda
Ice to fill four lowball glasses
2–3 sage leaves per glass for garnish

The crushed berries of Oregon grape stain your hands inky, but their bright purple juice is sour and so fun to play with in the kitchen. It tastes a bit like pomegranate juice when sweetened. Oregon grape is the Pacific Northwest coast's answer to lemon, so replace any call for lemon in a recipe with an equal amount of the berry juice. Turn your cake icing pink or make a cheerful white wine spritzer by adding a teaspoon or two. It's a prickly business harvesting the ripe deep purple berries in late July after their yellow flowers disappear. The holly-like spiky leaves protect the berries, but the harvest is well worth the effort.

(continued on page 125)

SIMPLE SYRUP

Place 2 parts Oregon grape juice to 1 part sugar in a Mason jar and shake until fully combined. Store in the fridge and use to make lemonade or sodas or as a cocktail sweetener.

COCKTAIL

Mix all the ingredients except the sage in a pitcher with ice, stir, and then pour into lowball glasses. Add a big ice cube and then smack or bruise the sage leaves to release their aroma and garnish the drinks with them.

› To get the grape juice, pick 4 cups (1 L) ripe purple Oregon grape berries and discard the stems. Wash the berries, add 2 cups (500 mL) cold water, then pulse them for 30 seconds in a food processor to release the juice. Pour into a sieve and press with the back of a spoon to extract the juice. Discard the pulp and seeds. Skim off any foam. The amount of juice you get will vary depending on the rainfall at time of harvest. I recommend picking more berries to make sure you get enough juice.

› Add more syrup to your taste if you want a sweeter drink.

FALL

Fall: Down the rabbit hole we go . . .

Toward the end of summer, an aura of melancholy seems to hang in the newly cool air. Long, warm days are now a memory and some people get a little sad. For me, the cooler weather and first fall rains are a time of anticipation, as another wild and wonderful mushroom hunting season is about to begin. I remember glorious mushroom years, like back in 2015, when everywhere you looked, colorful little heads poked out of the green moss. Many were types of mushrooms that I hadn't seen in years. I felt like Alice in Wonderland. When you're a chef, finding a new or rare ingredient can make you feel like a pirate unearthing a hidden treasure. Some mushrooms are eye-catching and make a great addition to any menu; they can smell like anise, flowers, cinnamon, or seafood and taste spicy, bitter, or addictively savory. These culinary gems are what make me so excited for the rain and happy to go out and get drenched in the forest anytime.

One particular year stands out for mushroom foraging for me. I was hiking with my dad near Vernon, BC. We found dozens of huge, fire engine–red lobster mushrooms beckoning to us like Christmas lights. Lobster mushrooms by design mimic the pods in the film *Invasion of the Body Snatchers*. Their spores (mushroom "seeds") float along until they attach themselves to a particular species of mushroom, like the large white mushroom *Russula brevipes*. The invader then proceeds to take over and turn its host mushroom lobster red in color and shapeshifts it into a blobby, gill-less form, which exudes a pungent seafood aroma as it ages. Lobster mushrooms are a surprisingly tasty mushroom, firm in texture with a unique seafood note. I have sautéed them and added them to pasta sauce, served them on steak, and fried them in butter for lunchtime toast with goat cheese and fresh herbs.

That same exciting, fruitful year, there were buckets of other edible mushrooms like shrimp Russula, another funky-colored purple mushroom that can grow as large as your hand and smells like shrimp paste, hedgehog mushrooms, big cream colored mushrooms with spines instead of gills, wacky neon yellow and orange chicken of the woods mushrooms that grow in layered shelves on old stumps, and bear's head (*Hericium abietis*) mushrooms, which decompose dead wood and look like clusters of bright white tiny icicles. Each month from

early August to late November where I am at the 49th parallel reveals new edible species to examine and then learn to cook with. Some turn out to be flavorless or too tough to be much use in my kitchen, but part of the fun is in the nibbling, poaching, sautéeing, and drying experimentation. I add new mushrooms to my pantry every year and enjoy expanding my culinary repertoire. The world of fungi is a deep, mysterious one. Even if you never harvest, I highly recommend you take the time to slowly study the forest floor and discover some of its secrets this fall.

CHANTERELLE MUSHROOM STUFFING

Makes 1 (9- × 13-inch/23 × 33 cm) casserole dish (enough to stuff an average turkey)

4 cups (1 L) sliced chanterelles
½ cup (125 mL) butter
2 celery stalks or fennel, diced
⅓ cup (80 mL) minced green onion
2 garlic cloves, chopped fine
3 sage leaves, chopped fine
¼ cup (60 mL) parsley, diced fine
1 Tbsp (15 mL) thyme leaves
Salt and pepper
1 cup (250 mL) Thompson or golden raisins or chopped apples
1 small loaf of sourdough bread, chopped into ¾-inch (2 cm) cubes
¼ cup (60 mL) olive oil
1–3 cups (250–750 mL) chicken or vegetable stock
9 very thin slices of de-seeded lemon or preserved lemons (page 106)
3 Tbsp (45 mL) chopped green onions, for topping

Pacific golden chanterelles fruit in October and November, depending on where you are along the coast, just in time for Thanksgiving. The deep pumpkin-orange mushrooms poke their heads out of the forest soil, just waiting for me to pick them. There is no better scavenger hunt than weaving my way between old Douglas-fir trees, scanning the soft, mossy ground for flashes of orange and filling my basket. I'm a popular family member when I manage to make this crowd-pleasing wild mushroom stuffing at Thanksgiving. If you find chanterelles earlier in the year, the best way to preserve them is to slice and fry them in oil, then freeze them, capturing more of their amazing aromatics.

Preheat the oven to 375°F.

Heat a large frying pan over medium-high heat for a minute or 2. Add the chanterelles and butter, cover and cook, stirring occasionally, for 5 minutes, then remove the lid to crisp and brown the mushrooms, about 5 minutes. Add the celery, minced green onions, garlic, sage, parsley, and thyme, and cook, stirring occasionally, until the vegetables begin to soften, 3–4 minutes. Season with salt and pepper to taste and stir in the raisins.

Toss the bread in the oil, season with salt, place on a rimmed baking tray, and crisp in the oven until brown, about 10 minutes.

Pour 1 cup (250 mL) of stock into a large bowl, add the bread, and let soften. Add the mushroom mixture to the bread and toss to combine.

(continued on page 133)

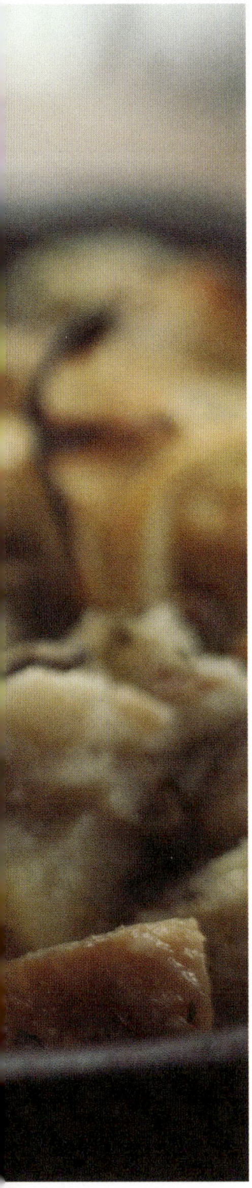

Preheat the oven to 425°F.

If you're baking the stuffing in a casserole dish, transfer it to a 9- × 13-inch (23 × 33 cm) dish and add enough stock to make the mixture quite moist. Top with the lemon slices and cover with aluminum foil. Bake for 25 minutes then uncover and finish cooking it on broil till the top is golden brown, about 5 minutes. Top with the chopped green onions before serving.

If you're baking the stuffing in a bird, once it's cooked, scoop out the stuffing, place it in a serving dish and top with the lemon. Sprinkle with the chopped green onions and serve hot.

› This recipe can be made with any firm mushroom and stuffed into any bird any day of the year. Other good candidates are morels, lobster mushrooms, or hedgehog mushrooms.

› If you are baking the stuffing in a bird rather than a casserole, you'll only need around 1 cup (250 mL) of stock.

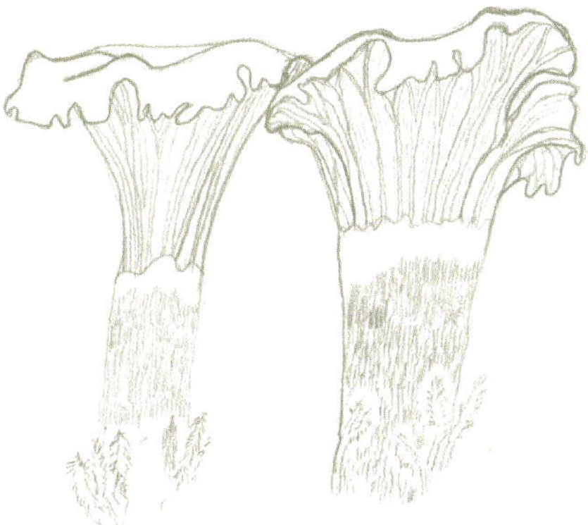

UNI BUTTER (GF)

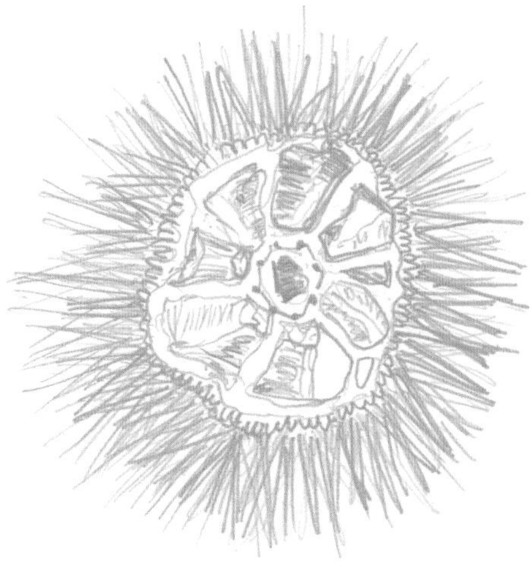

Makes 1½ cups (375 mL)

½ cup (125 mL) sea urchin roe (uni), about 2 live urchins
1 lb (454 g) butter, softened

In late spring and early fall, I harvest abundant prickly, red sea urchins at low tides in my wetsuit. The water can be crystal clear in the colder months, and you can spot urchin through the green and yellow-brown seaweed swaying gently to a spooky beat. Wonderfully, you can eat urchins all year round. You'll find when you crack one open that each urchin will usually have five delicious roe inside its shell and not much else. I tend to select younger urchins that have startlingly bright lemon-yellow to orange-red "roe." The roe in this case is actually the urchins' gonads. Sea urchins are weird and wonderful tasting. They're like the Parmesan of the sea: creamy, salty, and packed with umami. Easily worth braving the cold.

(*continued on page 137*)

Butchering the urchin might make some people squeamish, but I think it's an important step in learning about the food we choose to eat. North America as a culture is so removed from the fact that seafood indeed has to be killed to be eaten, that moments like these encourage you to make a fully informed choice about being a carnivore. Crack open the live sea urchin by cutting in a circle around the mouth, insert two spoons and lever the shell so that it splits in two. Carefully scrape any darker thin skin or seaweed debris out of the shell, taking care not to damage the roe. Once the debris is cleared away, scoop the brightly colored roe from the shell and place it in a bowl, making sure there are no broken spines in the bowl. Put the uni in a blender and mix on high speed with the room temperature butter until smooth. Put the uni butter into an airtight plastic container and refrigerate immediately to set it. Spread it on toast to serve with chowder or use as a simple sauce for cooked pasta.

› Uni is Japanese for urchin roe.

› If you harvest live urchin, eat a few roe raw for the sheer pleasure of it. If they are very rich, squeeze some lime on them. The roe will come in a gorgeous range of colors, from lemon yellow to reddish, and sizes depending on their age. I find about one in ten uni fresh from the sea have a slight taste of copper, but most are creamy and delicious, especially smaller urchin.

UNI BUTTER SAUCE WITH PASTA

Serves 4

¼ cup (60 mL) finely diced onion
1 tsp (5 mL) chili flakes (or more to your spice level)
4 Tbsp (60 mL) butter
4 cups (500 mL) chopped spinach
1 cup (250 mL) thinly sliced cauliflower
½ cup (60 mL) uni butter (page 134)
1 recipe homemade tagliatelle (page 34)
Salt
3 chopped tomatillos
1 lime, juiced and zested
½ cup (125 mL) grated pecorino cheese, for sprinkling (optional)

One summer a ways back, I worked for the winemakers Marilyn Schulze and Giordano Venturi in Cowichan Bay on the east coast of Vancouver Island, while I was studying viticulture (read: doing a lot of hand pruning and training of grapevines, as well as knocking down live wasp nests and getting stung in the eye!). Giordano would hand-make pasta to serve with his gorgeous ripe pinot noirs. I commented in my youthfulness, "I never make pasta. It's too much time and work." He just stared blankly at me, and I understood that I was missing the point. After that, I started learning to make pasta and now would attest that it actually doesn't take that long. Think about it: If you make handmade pasta, all you really need is butter and lemon juice to make it delicious, so you save time on that, and it is quite the showstopper at dinner.

Bring a pot of water to boil over high heat and salt it until it tastes like the sea.

Meanwhile, in a saucepan, cook the onions and chili flakes in the butter on medium heat for 3 minutes. Turn the heat to low, add the spinach, cauliflower, uni butter, and a pinch of salt and cook for 1 minute, just to soften the vegetables. Turn off the heat.

Drop the pasta into the boiling water, stir to loosen the pasta up, and boil for 1–2 minutes. Taste a piece to see if it's done. When it's done, drain the pasta, but reserve ½ cup (125 mL) of the cooking water. Add the lime juice and zest to the saucepan and then use the pasta water to thin the uni butter sauce if necessary. Taste, then add more plain butter or pasta water if you want to mellow the flavor. Toss the pasta in the sauce. Serve topped with pecorino, tomatillos, and more chili flakes if you wish.

WILD MUSHROOM PÂTÉ (GF)

Makes 1 loaf

1½ cups (375 mL) chicken or vegetable stock
1 cup (250 mL) dried porcini mushrooms (1 oz/25 g)
½ cup (125 mL) butter, divided
¾ cup (180 mL) minced onion
2 garlic cloves, minced
¼ cup (60 mL) amontillado (or your favorite medium sherry)
¾ lb (340 g) wild mushrooms like chanterelles, thinly sliced
¾ lb (340 g) oyster mushrooms, thinly sliced
4 large eggs
¼ cup (60 mL) toasted pumpkin seeds, ground
¼ cup (60 mL) chopped Italian parsley
2 tsp (10 mL) chopped thyme leaves
1 cup (250 mL) heavy cream
⅓ cup (80 mL) fine cornmeal
2 tsp (10 mL) salt
½ tsp (2.5 mL) pepper
1½ Tbsp (22 mL) lemon juice

Our wild mushroom foraging classes fill up in fall with hungry hikers. This is a time to enjoy the dark, rainy months by pulling on your rainboots, breathing in the crisp, forest air, and discovering where to find the fattest porcini and the most intoxicatingly aromatic matsutake among a host of other edible and fascinating fungi. I sometimes serve this mushroom pâté to my students as food inspiration. We gather around the picnic table and treat ourselves to a hearty spread of pâté, seaweed bread, and truffled feta, while warming our hands on a mug of hot, wild forest tea. What a perfect way to kick-start a journey into the forest to find your own edible treats.

Bring the stock to a boil in a small saucepan over high heat. Remove the pan from the heat. Add the dried porcini to the hot stock to soak until softened, about 30 minutes. Using a slotted spoon, transfer the porcini to a food processor fitted with the steel blade and blend until smooth. Sieve the stock to remove any grit, then bring it to a simmer over medium heat and cook until reduced to about ¼ cup (60 mL), about 10 minutes. Stir this into the blended porcini.

Preheat the oven to 350°F. Grease a 4½- × 8½-inch (11 × 22 cm) loaf pan.

Heat 2 Tbsp (30 mL) of the butter in a large, deep skillet on medium heat. Add the onions and garlic and cook, stirring, until softened, 6 minutes. Transfer to a large bowl and set aside. Add the rest of the butter to the skillet along with the sherry and sliced mushrooms, cover and cook for 5 minutes. Uncover and cook, stirring occasionally, until the mushrooms are browned, 10–15 minutes. Blend the onion, sautéed mushrooms, and porcini mixture in your food processor until roughly

(continued on page 145)

puréed. Add the eggs, pumpkin seeds, parsley, thyme, and cream to the food processor and purée until combined. Using a spoon, stir in the cornmeal, salt, pepper, and lemon juice. Taste to make sure the pâté is salted enough. Pour mixture into the prepared pan and cover with foil.

Bake until set, about 40–50 minutes. The pâté will look wet in the middle, but it should come away from the pan edges slightly. Remove the pan from the oven and let cool to room temperature. Cover the pan and refrigerate the pâté for at least 6 hours to set further. Bring it to room temperature before serving. Spread on toasts or crackers.

› For a delicious alternative, slice and fry 10 large chanterelles in 3 Tbsp (45 mL) of butter. Spread them overtop the pâté and sprinkle with some cracked salt. This will keep in an airtight container in the fridge for about 1 week.

PASTA WITH PORCINI AND LEMON CREAM

Serves 4

PORCINI SAUCE

1½ cups (375 mL) chicken or vegetable stock
¾ cup (180 mL) dried porcini
1 tsp (5 mL) flour or cornstarch
Salt and pepper
3 whole juniper berries, finely ground (optional)

LEMON CREAM SAUCE

1 Tbsp (15 mL) butter
1 Tbsp (15 mL) finely diced onion
½ cup (125 mL) dry white wine (Sauvignon Blanc is good)
¾ cup (180 mL) whipping cream
2 tsp (10 mL) thyme
2 Tbsp (30 mL) lemon juice
½ tsp (2.5 mL) lemon zest
Salt and pepper
¼ cup (60 mL) grated Parmigiano-Reggiano, for garnish

PASTA

1 recipe nettle pasta (page 34)

Porcini signify the start of mushroom season. They can pop up in August and into the early fall (*Boletus edulis*) which makes me want to run outside and peek under every pine, spruce, fir, and hemlock! You can find porcini in spring as well. These types of porcini are called spring kings and are a different species (*Boletus rex-veris*). They are very large and delicious. When I find a young firm porcini I like to fry it up in a hot dry pan (no oil, just salt). Older mushrooms should be sliced and dehydrated or made into sauces.

PORCINI SAUCE

Bring the stock to a boil in a small saucepan over high heat. Remove the pan from the heat. Add the dried porcini and let soak until softened, about 20 minutes. Using a slotted spoon, remove the porcini from the stock, chop roughly, and set aside. Sieve the stock to remove any grit.

Put the flour in a small bowl and whisk in 2 Tbsp (30 mL) of water. Whisking constantly, slowly add the stock. Make sure there are no lumps. If you do end up with lumps, just sieve the stock again. Return the stock to the pot to heat on medium-high to thicken and reduce until you have a gravy consistency, about 10 minutes. Add salt and pepper to taste and the juniper berries (if using).

Bring a big pot of heavily salted water to boil in preparation for cooking your pasta.

LEMON CREAM SAUCE

Cook the butter and onion in a saucepan over medium heat, 2 minutes. Add the wine, turn the heat to high, and cook until the wine is reduced by half, 2 minutes. Stir in the cream and thyme and reduce the heat to a simmer for 5 minutes until it thickens to a gravy consistency. Add the lemon juice, lemon zest, salt, and pepper to taste.

(*continued on page 148*)

PASTA

Add the pasta to the pot of boiling water and cook until al dente (2–4 minutes for fresh pasta, depending on thickness).

To serve, drizzle lemon cream sauce and then porcini sauce over the pasta, then top with the chopped porcini and Parmigiano-Reggiano.

> I always think about timing when cooking for guests. Cream sauces and cooked pasta are best served as soon as possible so they don't curdle or clump, so getting your salted pasta water boiling early is a good practice.

> You can use the nettle pasta recipe from this cookbook or use a peeler to make strips of raw carrot and blanch them for 2 minutes in hot water for a gluten-free option. (If you want to make this gluten-free, be sure to check the label of your cornstarch.) Or simply buy some fresh pasta if you prefer.

BRAISED BURDOCK ROOT CONGEE (GF)

Serves 6

BURDOCK

2 Tbsp (30 mL) sesame oil
1 clove garlic, minced
2 cups (500 mL) burdock, peeled and chopped into ¼-inch (1 cm) dice
¾ cup (180 mL) water
6 Tbsp (90 mL) soy sauce
3 Tbsp (45 mL) ponzu sauce
½ tsp (2.5 mL) pepper

CONGEE

1 cup (250 mL) jasmine rice, rinsed
1 handful of dried sliced porcini mushrooms (or shiitake)
6 cups (1.5 L) chicken or vegetable stock
2 Tbsp (30 mL) light soy sauce
2 Tbsp (30 mL) fish sauce

TOPPINGS

2 tsp (10 mL) fried diced garlic (see page 86)
4 tsp (20 mL) grated ginger
2 tsp (10 mL) cilantro

It's easiest to harvest burdock root in the plant's first fall or second spring. It is a tenacious plant that loves hard-packed soil at the sides of paths and will grow almost anywhere across North America. To dig the tap root, you'll need a good shovel and some elbow grease. Its nutty flavor is well worth the effort, and you can eat it raw or cooked.

Cooked burdock is always the main topping when I make congee. During my time in Thailand studying cooking, I ate a lot of the savory breakfast called jok, which is basically Thai congee. You can make congee from scratch or use day-old rice. One Thai cook showed me a great tweak to the recipe where you pulse yesterday's rice with a bit of the water in a blender first to produce a broken rice texture which is really nice.

(continued on page 153)

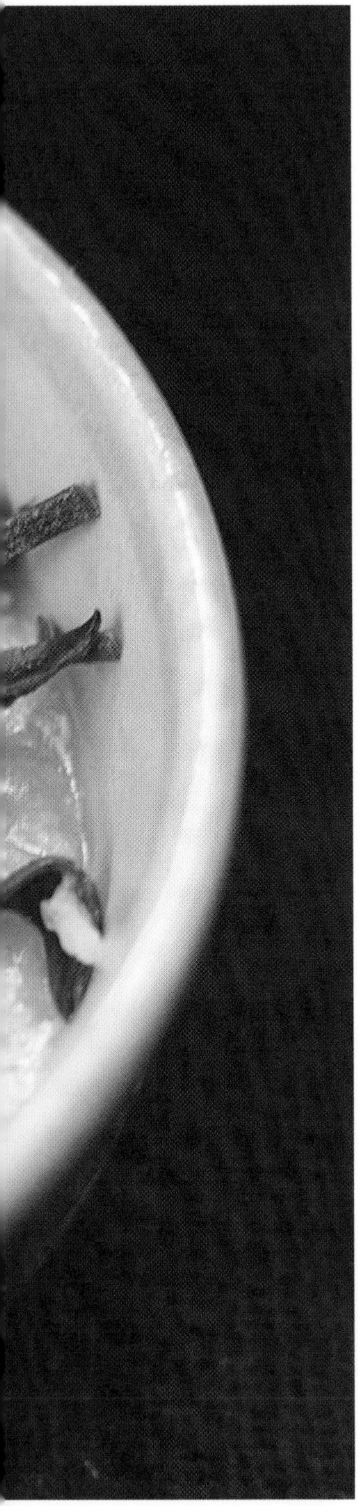

BURDOCK

Heat the oil in a medium pot over medium heat. Add the garlic and burdock and cook for 30 seconds. Stir in the water, soy sauce, ponzu, and pepper, cover and turn the heat down to low. Cook, stirring once or twice, until the burdock is tender, about 30 minutes. Keep the burdock covered with liquid while it cooks. You may need to add some more water.

CONGEE

Put all the congee ingredients into a large heavy-bottomed pot and bring to a boil over high heat. Cover and turn down the heat to simmer. Stir regularly until the rice has cooked into a porridge consistency, about 45 minutes. Add more fish sauce, if needed, as you would salt.

Top with burdock, garlic, ginger, and cilantro and serve for breakfast or lunch. Any leftovers can be put in the fridge and reheated the next day with a little water to thin.

› If you can't find any wild burdock, don't despair. You can always look in an Asian grocery store (where you'll also find fried garlic).

› You can add many different ingredients to your bowl of congee, but don't skip the fried garlic and fresh ginger added at the end. Try adding various amounts of cooked chicken or fried mushrooms, chopped green onions, bean sprouts, chili oil, Chinese vinegar, pea shoots, shredded prosciutto, fresh chili, fresh lemon, fried garlic or braised daikon (use the same method for cooking as the burdock), and one poached egg per person.

FORAGER'S FRUIT PIE

Makes 2 (10-inch/ 25 cm) pies

GRANDMA RUTH'S CRUST

8 oz (226 g) ice-cold vegetable shortening or lard
2¾ cups (680 mL) flour
½ beaten egg
1 tsp (5 mL) vinegar
½ tsp (2.5 mL) salt
¾ cup (180 mL) cold water
1 beaten egg, for brushing

APPLE PIE FILLING (1 pie)

4 cups (1 L) wild apples, cored, peeled, and sliced (¼-inch/ ½ cm thick)
½ cup (125 mL) packed brown sugar (adjust depending on how sour your apples are)
1 Tbsp (15 mL) flour
1 tsp (5 mL) lemon zest
Pinch of salt
½ tsp (2.5 mL) grated ginger or crushed juniper berries

A gnarled apple tree grew wild in a corner of Stanley Park in Vancouver, BC, when I was a kid. My dad would harvest the beaten-looking apples and my mom would use them to make a forager's pie. Sour wild apples are perfect for baking. The contrast of sweet and sour with a rich ice cream melting over a warm crust is what dreams are made of. Another classic in my family is my grandmother's summer saskatoon berry pie. Saskatoons grow best in the Canadian prairies, but you can find them on the coast too, and in some years they can taste up to par. They taste a bit like a blueberry with a unique clove-like note. Grandma would assemble four or five pies at once and then freeze some unbaked. Whenever she felt like having a pie, she would let them thaw for 45 minutes or so and then pop them in the oven to bake "'til they looked right."

GRANDMA RUTH'S CRUST

Cut the cold shortening into the flour with a pastry blender or fork until it makes a pea-sized crumble.

Beat together the ½ egg, vinegar, and salt in a measuring cup. Add enough ice-cold water to reach the ¾ cup (180 mL) mark. Add this mixture slowly and evenly to the flour, tossing continuously with a fork making sure it's evenly moist. Add just enough to make a ball of dough that holds together. If it's too wet the crust will be tough. Try not to handle the dough too much as your warm hands will melt the fat. Divide it into 4 loosely packed balls, wrap in plastic, and chill in the fridge for 15 minutes.

Dust your work surface and rolling pin well with flour. Note that overworking your pastry will make it tough. Use flour to dust whenever the dough appears to be sticking. You can use a floured pastry scraper

(continued on page 157)

SASKATOON BERRY PIE FILLING (1 pie)

4 cups (1 L) saskatoon berries
2 Tbsp (30 mL) lemon juice
½ cup (125 mL) packed brown sugar
2½ Tbsp (35 mL) corn starch

or flat spatula to scrape up the dough if you find it's sticking to the work surface. Roll out 2 balls of the dough into a rough circle. Drape each one over a 10-inch (25 cm) pie dish. (If you're only making one pie, roll out 1 ball of dough, put one aside for the top crust, and put the other two in the freezer to use another time.)

FILLING

Preheat the oven to 425°F.

Mix together the ingredients of your chosen pie filling and put them into your pie crusts after you roll them out.

Wet the rim of the pastry shell with a bit of water to help seal the edges. Roll out the last two balls of dough for the top crusts. Cover each pie with a top crust and press the rim with your finger to seal. Use a knife to trim off excess dough from around the edges. Cut an X in the center of the pie to release steam. Brush the crust with the egg to help with browning. Bake the two pies side by side in the middle of the oven on a baking tray to catch any filling that bubbles over.

After 15 minutes, reduce the temperature to 350°F and continue baking until the filling is soft and the crust is browned, 35–45 minutes. For apples, you can test how cooked they are by inserting a knife into the vent hole to check that they are soft. For a berry pie, skip this step as they soften faster. Grandma just baked hers at 350°F for around 50 minutes, so try that if you want a lighter brown crust.

› Half a beaten egg should be 1 oz (28 g). Whisk an egg well and then split it into two equal portions by eye.

› You may know saskatoons as service berries.

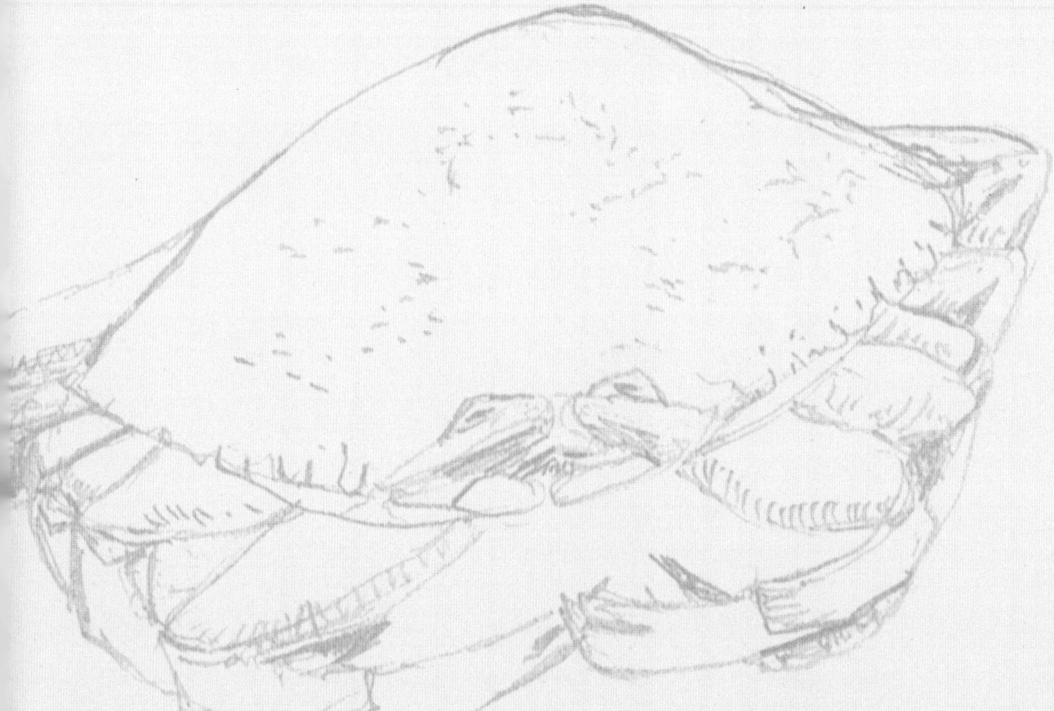

WINTER

Winter foraging by the sea

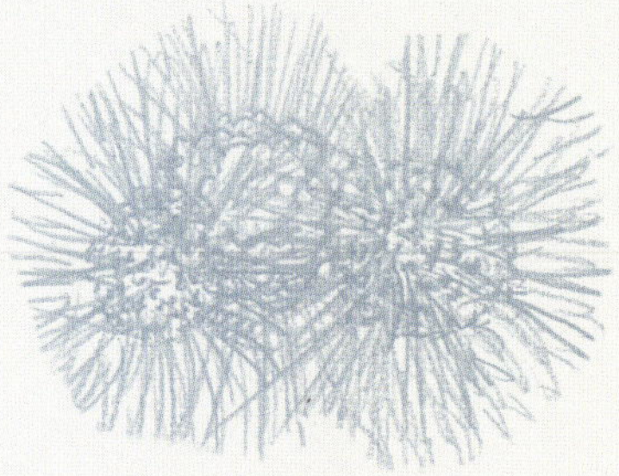

The ocean is your best bet for a delicious harvest in winter, and knowing its offerings well could help you survive the next zombie apocalypse. I always have a nice fire going at my cabin before heading out to dive for sea urchin, sea cucumber, and crab. The shoreline where I fish is rocky and covered with the sharp little shells of edible thatched barnacles, among other tasty creatures like sea snails, oysters, mussels, and limpets. Limpet ceviche is always a surprise hit. Don't knock it until you try it! Shellfish are usually most delicious in winter when you can shuck oysters right off the rocks—no need for ice. The worst time to harvest shellfish, in my mind, is summer when they get funky-tasting from both spawning and the warmer water with potential muddy river outflow. Red rock crab is sometimes within grabbing distance on a low tide—just watch your fingers and pick them up from the back side or top of their shell. In a few hours, I can have a bag full of tasty treats ready for the pot. The cold water keeps many people at bay, but it holds the highest-quality seafood. Winter is, of course, the least comfortable time for swimming, so wise folk go at low tide to minimize dive depths. Slipping into a full wetsuit (if you have one) staves off the freezing water for a while. When my head plunges into the sea, the water hits my ears and I always get a sharp, breath-sucking shock from the icy water. It takes a second to get my game face back on and I have to breathe deep and slow to calm down. Under the water, I can see dozens of red and purple spiny urchins quilting the shear rock face. The urchin carpet extends as far as I can see until they disappear into a deep, dark blue abyss 150-plus feet straight down. Floating in the tossing waves, I relax into the rocking motion and time my dives with the waves so I don't get bashed into the cliffs. The sea urchins suction themselves hard to the rocks, so I have a long knife to pry them off and tongs to grab them. This method is perhaps a little less elegant than that used by some Indigenous peoples to harvest urchin, with a long three-pronged spear, but it gets the job done.

Sea urchin is such a delicacy and there is nothing like surfacing with your catch and cracking the spiny shell open to eat the savory, rich roe. Urchin "roe" is called skuē' tsai by the Squamish (Sḵwx̱wú7mesh) Peoples of the region and you may recognize it as uni (in Japanese). It is a true gift from the sea.

I'm always incredibly hungry after being out in cold water, so making a quick kelp and smoked fish broth (dashi stock) is a simple way to cook any catch from clams to crab, hot pot style, to feed gathered friends. Serve the feast with bread, butter, chili, and lime, and remember to thank the ocean (and the urchin!).

ROASTED POPWEED (GF)

Makes 4 cups (1 L)

4 cups (1 L) popweed

Popweed (also called rockweed, bladderwrack, or ts'alh) grows on practically every sheltered rock in the intertidal zone of the Pacific Northwest. It's so common you almost don't realize it's there. Kids play with it, popping the bladders at the beach. Many will never know how much of an ally to humans this seaweed can be. It's a mild sunscreen, good for the skin, and delicious roasted. I like the ones with puffy pouches best, because they have more crunch once they're roasted. Rinse popweed in clean sea water after harvesting to release any baby snails or small critters back into the ocean.

After you harvest the popweed, let it dry out in the sun for 12 hours before roasting. This speeds up the cooking process.

Preheat the oven to 350°F. Line a cookie sheet with parchment paper.

Spread the popweed evenly on the parchment paper in a single layer and bake until the thickest part of the popweed is cracker-crisp, about 20–30 minutes, depending on how dry it is at the start. Let cool and then place in an airtight container lined with paper towel.

Serve these as a component of dashi hot pot (page 186), on rice, or in salad. Make sure to add the popweed at the last minute so it keeps its crunch.

LAPHROAIG CLAM CHOWDER (GF)

Serves 4

2 lb (900 g) Manila clams
1½ cups (375 mL) water
1 medium onion, diced
½ cup (125 mL) diced fennel, fronds reserved for garnish
¾ cup (175 mL) diced celery ribs
¼ cup (60 mL) diced carrot
2 Tbsp (30 mL) butter
1¼ cups (310 mL) chicken stock
¾ cup (175 mL) diced red potatoes
1 bay leaf
½ tsp (2.5 mL) anchovy paste
½ tsp (2.5 mL) saffron threads (optional)
Pinch of celery salt
10 oz (280 g) salmon, cut in ¾-inch (2 cm) cubes
1 (14 oz/418 g) can creamed corn
1 cup (250 mL) 2% milk (or chicken stock)
¼ cup (60 mL) Laphroaig whisky (or another peaty variety)
Salt and pepper
2 tsp (20 mL) fried garlic (see page 86), for garnish

I love bringing this chowder to the beach already cooked. After a day of crab fishing, I steam up any crab we caught in the soup. But even if we don't catch any crab, we still have lunch to eat. This recipe is very versatile, so you can add whatever seafood you harvest to it: clams, mussels, cod, salmon, scallops, prawns, or shrimp. Crab is best caught in cooler months, and chowder is the perfect warm-up on a crisp day. Serve it with uni butter (page 134) on good bread for a decadent accent.

If you've harvested the clams yourself, make sure you purge them before cooking to remove any grit and mud (see page 176). Then prepare the clams as described on page 178.

Place the water in a deep, wide pot and bring to a boil over high heat. Add the clams, cover the pot, and steam for 3 minutes. The clams should all have popped open. If any haven't opened, cook them for a few minutes longer until they do. Transfer the clams to a bowl and let cool. Reserve the cooking liquid.

(*continued on page 168*)

Using the same pot (no need to clean it out first), sauté the onions, fennel, celery, and carrots in the butter over medium heat until soft, about 5 minutes. Add the reserved cooking water and stock, followed by the potatoes, bay leaf, anchovy paste, saffron, and celery salt. Cover and cook on medium-high until the potatoes are cooked, about 15 minutes. Stir in the salmon, creamed corn, and milk, and cook for 15 minutes. Stir in the whisky last and season to taste with salt and pepper.

Divide the clams between four bowls and pour the soup overtop. Garnish with fried garlic and some fennel fronds or flowers and serve hot with bread and butter.

› Switch the chicken stock for crab broth, made simply by simmering crab shells in water for 45 minutes. Smoked shellfish works really well in this recipe in place of the clams.

› Cook broken-down crab legs in the broth until the flesh is white, about 15 minutes, and use in addition to the clams.

BAKED WINE AND GARLIC CRAB (GF)

Serves 4

4 (each 1½–2 lb/680–900 g) live Dungeness crabs
4 cloves minced organic garlic (or 6 cloves regular garlic)
¼ cup (60 mL) butter
¼ cup (60 mL) water
3 Tbsp (45 mL) dry white wine (Sauvignon Blanc is perfect) or lemon juice

Learning to cast for crab from the docks at Jericho Beach was a foraging rite of passage for me. Crabbing is all about the throw. The farther you throw your trap, the deeper the water and the bigger the crab. When I first started crabbing, I was one of the few women at the dock. I remember one crabber called Superman. We called him that because when he wound up and threw, it seemed like his trap would hit the tankers moored way out in the harbor. Occasionally, Superman would even grab my trap after I baited it and throw it out into the water, uh...ok. Well, it wasn't long before I was throwing out into deep water, too, ha. We couldn't communicate as much as we would have liked to because of the language barrier, but everyone who caught a big crab off the docks got a knowing nod from Superman. Chatting with friendly strangers and whiling away a lazy day on the dock catching crab always brought me moments of welcome interaction and reflection.

I first butchered a live crab with my uncle and aunt. It is not for the faint of heart, but it does require you to make a distinct choice and respect the animal that you will be consuming by making its death a quick one. I never boil crab. You lose all that great crab taste to the water, which is also true to a lesser degree with steaming. When you cook crab my way, you'll be steaming it in its own juices and the crab will taste like true gold, with that garlic butter magic aroma that makes you want to release your inner caveman and crack some shells.

(continued on page 173)

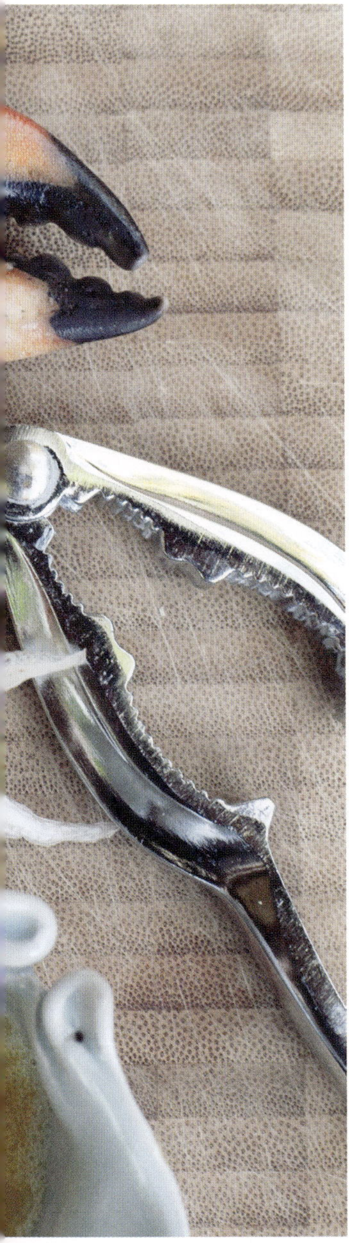

Butcher your crab. This is the hard part for most people. The easiest way to do it is to flip the crab on its back and just cut it in half with a confident swing of a sharp, heavy butcher knife. Or you can position the crab on its belly and pull the carapace (head shell) off by holding one side of the crab down by the legs. Then, break the crab in half, being careful of the big front claws. Strip the triangular gray gills off the body with a knife (optional). Cut the legs into manageable pieces and tap them with a hammer to crack and make them easier to eat later. Place the pieces body side down in a deep pot with the carapaces on top of all the meat to trap the steam and flavor the butter. The yellowish organs in the carapace are the crab butter which is a delicacy that adds flavor to any dish.

Cook, covered, with all the other ingredients on medium-high heat until the crab meat turns from translucent to white, 15–20 minutes.

Divide the meat between four bowls and pour in the crabby jus. You can let the jus soak the crab meat or sop it up with bread.

› Squeeze the crab's back leg gently to make sure the shell is rock-hard. This ensures that the crab has completed molting and the meat has grown fully into the shell. If the shell is soft, there will be less meat in the body.

› You can also use local red rock crab in this recipe. The shells are harder but the meat is sweeter. They tend to be smaller than Dungeness, so you may have to use one extra to get the same amount of crab meat.

SHERRY-SMOKED BLUE MUSSELS (GF)

Serves 4

4 lb (2 kg) mussels
1 cup (250 mL) amontillado (medium sherry)
1 cup (250 mL) water
1 large garlic clove, crushed
¼ cup (60 mL) extra virgin olive oil or hazelnut oil
2 Tbsp (30 mL) finely chopped fresh evergreen tips or rosemary leaves (optional)

I find myself returning to Barcelona, Spain, like a culinary homing pigeon every few years. I spend my time there cooking, sipping vermut de casa in the plazas, spending hours in the food markets, and devouring the coastal Mediterranean dishes. The influence of Spain has seeped into my recipes as many ingredients are so similar to those of my home, especially the shellfish. These smoked mussels are no exception. Serve them with toasted garlic bread and a glass of amontillado, a medium sherry that is just lightly sweet and tastes of almonds and Spanish sunshine.

Tap the shell of any open mussels. If they don't move, discard them. Closed live mussels show you they are alive by holding their shells tightly shut; there's no need to tap them. Rinse and scrub the mussels to remove any debris. (You'll cut the beard—the stringy, hairy bits—off after you steam the mussels.)

Bring the amontillado, water, and garlic to a boil in a wide, deep covered pan on high heat. Add some mussels in a single layer, cover and steam until they open, 2–3 minutes. Move the cooked mussels to a bowl and add another batch to steam. Repeat until you've steamed all the mussels. Mussels that remain closed just need to be steamed longer until they open up even a little as their inner muscle is still holding the shell shut. When you are done, pour the mussel broth into another large bowl slowly, leaving any debris settled at the bottom of the pot to be discarded.

(*continued on page 176*)

Shuck the mussels, using a spoon to remove them from their shells. Use scissors to cut off any beard. Then drop each mussel into the strained broth to soak for 20 minutes.

Fire up a smoker to about 145°F. Alder is the best wood for this recipe. Use a fine grate so the mussels don't fall through.

Smoke the mussels for 30 minutes. Don't let the smoker get too hot! When they are done, toss the mussels in the oil and evergreen tips (if using). Eat hot, or store in an airtight glass jar in the fridge for up to 1 week. Freeze what you don't eat or use them in a nice seafood soup.

› You can also use this recipe for other small clams like Manila clams. If you've dug the clams yourself, make sure you purge them in a plastic bucket of cold seawater for at least an hour, to a maximum of 20 hours, before cooking to remove any grit and mud. There is no need to purge store-bought shellfish.

› Use a high-quality oil for best results.

GAPER CLAM CRUDO (GF)

Serves 4 as an appetizer

4 gaper clam siphons (about 1 cup/250 mL sliced)
1½ Tbsp (22 mL) lemon juice
1 lemon
1½ tsp (7.5 mL) good finishing olive oil
2 tsp (10 mL) chopped dill
1 tsp (5 mL) minced chives (or chive blossoms if you want to make it gorgeous)
1½ tsp (7.5 mL) tamari
Pinch of guajillo or ancho chili (optional)

Gaper clam, also called horse clam, is the lazy clam digger's geoduck. If you've never had geoduck, it's the Pacific Northwest's largest and most expensive clam. The gaper clam's sliced siphon (the long neck of a clam) is crunchy and very similar in flavor to geoduck, clean and rich-tasting. The bonus with gaper is that you only have to dig about a leisurely 2 feet (60 cm) down in the sand to find them, whereas geoduck can require more than 3 feet (1 meter) of sweat-soaked digging!

A variation of this recipe was introduced to me by my friend Hanako Maeda on a clam dig in Birch Bay, Washington, with a flock of wonderful clam diggers and chefs. It was a magical sunset evening, made better by the excellent food that we'd been gifted by the sea. If you are ever in the area, it's a great place to dig for butter clams and horse clams.

Rinse the clams and use a paring knife to remove the meat from the shell. Feel around to cut the muscles that hold it closed. Remove the clam meat and cut the siphon or neck of the clam where it attaches to the body meat. The body meat can be rinsed further to remove any sand or grit and chopped fine to add to a chowder or frozen for later use.

Prepare an ice bath.

Bring a pot of salted water or seawater to a boil and dip the siphons into the hot water for 1–2 minutes to loosen the skin. Plunge them into the ice bath, then peel the outer skin off the siphon. Slice the siphon in two lengthwise and then slice thin pieces of clam for your crudo. The fresher the clam, the better this dish will taste.

(continued on page 181)

Zest 1 tsp (5 mL) of lemon peel. Then, cut the lemon in half widthwise and remove the seeds. Cut one half into small, thin slices of lemon for presentation.

Place the clam in a large bowl and add the rest of the ingredients, including the zest. Squeeze the remaining half of the lemon onto the crudo, toss, and taste. Add more tamari if necessary and top the crudo with lemon slices and serve with a crisp white wine.

› Olive oil comes in many different flavors. For this recipe I prefer a greener olive oil, meaning the olives were harvested less ripe for a sharper flavor.

› Geoduck siphon could be prepared with this same recipe, but you'll only need one siphon because they are so large.

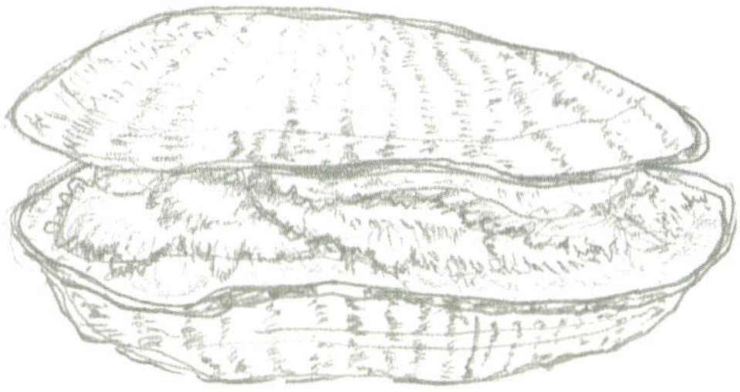

JUNIPER FISH STEW (GF)

Serves 4–6

2 garlic cloves, chopped
½ cup (125 mL) diced fennel
½ cup (125 mL) diced onion
½ cup (125 mL) frozen corn
½ cup (125 mL) diced russet potato (½-inch/1 cm pieces)
½ cup (125 mL) diced Savoy cabbage
¼ cup (60 mL) diced carrots
¼ cup (60 mL) diced celery
¼ cup (60 mL) diced zucchini
½ tsp (2 mL) pepper
4 Tbsp (60 mL) sunflower oil, divided
8 cups (2 L) chicken or fish stock (or dashi, page 186)
2 Tbsp (30 mL) fish sauce
12 oz (340 g) can crushed tomatoes
1¼ lb (560 g) ling cod, skin and bones removed, cut into ½-inch (1 cm) pieces
6 oz (170 g) salmon, cod, halibut, or shellfish per person, fish cut into ½-inch (1 cm) pieces
½ cup (125 mL) chopped celery leaves, for garnish
1 lime, sliced into wedges for garnish
1 Tbsp (15 mL) juniper berries, ground fine

Juniper is a Pacific Northwest herbal doppelganger for pepper or cloves. It's best added as a finishing spice because its zesty, piney aroma disappears quickly when cooked for too long. Juniper berries (which are actually cones) have been used in medicine and cooking for centuries, from Sweden to Oregon. The best time to harvest the berries is when they are ripe and dark blue. They can take a few years to ripen fully, so you have to have a patient soul. In Canada, juniper is commonly used to accent game meat, but it works as a great complement for lamb, pork, and strong-tasting fish like salmon too.

(*continued on page 184*)

Sauté the garlic, all the vegetables, and the pepper in 2 Tbsp (30 mL) of the oil over medium heat until soft, about 5 minutes. Mix in the stock, fish sauce, and tomatoes and bring to a boil, then turn down the heat to simmer.

Salt the fish and seafood pieces liberally. Heat the remaining 2 Tbsp (30 mL) oil on medium-high heat in a wide frying pan. Fry the fish in batches until brown, 1 minute per side, making sure not to overcrowd your pan.

Pour the soup into bowls and top with the cooked fish and seafood. Garnish with the celery leaves and sprinkle some ground juniper on top for a nice aroma before serving.

› In summer, I love buying a load of fresh sweet corn, slicing it off the cob, and freezing it. It's so much better than any frozen or canned corn you can buy in the store in winter.

DASHI HOT POT WITH MATSUTAKE (GF)

Serves 4

DASHI STOCK

- 2 (each 8 × 8 inches/ 20 × 20 cm) pieces fresh whole kombu or sugar kelp blades
- 4 cups (1 L) water
- ½ cup (125 mL) skipjack katsuobushi
- 3 Tbsp (45 mL) soy sauce (optional)
- Fish sauce (optional)

HOT POT

- 1 (4-inch/10 cm) tall matsutake mushroom, sliced paper thin
- 1 handful mizuna lettuce (or arugula)
- 2 oz (50 g) per person thin sliced raw beef (cuts like marbled ribeye or shoulder chuck have a good amount of marbling for this recipe)
- 2 oz (50 g) per person thinly sliced raw scallops
- ½ cup (125 mL) oven-roasted slices of kabocha squash
- 1 tsp (5 mL) roasted popweed per serving (page 162)

My first matsutake hunt was with a gaggle of friends in the Coast Mountains near Whistler, BC. I smelled the spicy aroma of the mushrooms before I saw them. There were dozens of full caps popping out from under the forest moss. We excitedly picked armfuls of this prized treasure and divided the spoils. It was like finding pirate booty. To find matsutake (also called pine mushrooms, *Tricholoma murrillanium*), you must know in your bones what they smell like as they have deadly poisonous lookalikes in some regions. One of their main identifying characteristics is their addictive scent of "Red Hots and dirty socks" or (put more pleasantly) of cinnamon and earth.

DASHI STOCK

Place the kombu and the water in a pot and bring it to a boil over high heat. Immediately turn the heat off and add the katsuobushi flakes. Don't stir. Let sit for 5 minutes and then strain the stock through a fine mesh sieve. This is your dashi base stock. Add the soy sauce and fish sauce to taste if you'd like to create a deeper flavor.

HOT POT

Divide the ingredients between four small bowls, placing them in a pretty pattern. Return the stock to the pot and bring to a boil. Present the bowls to your guests and pour the hot soup over the ingredients tableside for a flourish.

(continued on page 188)

OPTIONAL INGREDIENTS

(Amounts below are all per person)

- 1 oz (25 g) chopped braised burdock root or cooked daikon
- 1 oz (25 g) bullwhip kelp pickle
- 1 oz (25 g) raw sea asparagus
- 1 oz (25 g) snap peas
- 2 oz (50 g) fried cauliflower mushroom or lion's mane
- 2 oz (50 g) steamed yu choy or bok choy

› When you're buying katsuobushi, look for large flakes as they make a clearer stock.

› Dashi is a pure golden stock where every spoonful helps infuse your body with energy and nutrients. Simmered salty seaweed and smoked, dried fish cooked with care creates this gorgeous base stock that you can make miso soup from or turn into a tasty hot pot by adding thinly sliced meat, fish, or vegetables. It's a really fast recipe, easy to make for both large and small groups of hungry people. I first had this style of soup in Tokyo and immediately fell in love with it.

› Cut the beef semi-frozen to easily make very thin slices. Use Wagyu beef if you want to up your game.

› The hot broth cooks the raw meat and fish perfectly when you pour it over tableside, but if you leave the bowls too long the meat may get tough.

MUSSEL, HAZELNUT, AND GREEN PAPAYA SALAD (GF)

Serves 4

1 cup (250 mL) de-shelled smoked mussels
1 cup (250 mL) green papaya peeled, deseeded, and shredded
1 (10-inch/25 cm) raw burdock root, peeled and shredded
1 roasted red bell pepper, diced fine
1 clove roasted garlic, minced
1 large handful bean sprouts
2 green Thai chilies, deseeded and diced fine
¼ cup (60 mL) ground roasted hazelnuts
2 Tbsp (30 mL) minced green onions
2 Tbsp (30 mL) brown sugar or palm sugar
A few sprigs cilantro, minced
2 Tbsp (30 mL) lime juice or Oregon grape juice
2 Tbsp (30 mL) fish sauce
1 Tbsp (15 mL) hazelnut oil

The base for this recipe comes from Chiang-mai, Thailand, from Chef Panphailin Puntira, who taught me so much about Thai and Lanna cuisine. When I returned home, I played with creating a Pacific Northwest twist on this classic green papaya salad recipe since I loved it so much. Hazelnut replaced peanut, Oregon grape juice for lime, burdock for carrot, and smoked mussels for prawns. Enjoy!

Combine all the ingredients and then taste for balance. Add more fish sauce, sugar, or lime according to your palate.

› Most of the time for this recipe is spent on shredding, dicing, and mincing. You are welcome to use a grater or a mandolin to shred the vegetables, or practice your knife skills and chop very fine 2-inch (10 cm) long slices of your papaya and burdock.

AVGOLEMONO SOUP WITH TRUFFLES (GF)

Serves 6

3 Tbsp (45 mL) white vinegar
9 large eggs, divided
8 cups (2 L) chicken stock
1⅓ cups (330 mL) cooked arborio rice
5 Tbsp (75 mL) lemon juice (3 to 4 lemons)
Salt and white pepper
1 baguette, sliced
Extra virgin olive oil
Cracked salt
1 (1 oz/25 g) fresh white or black truffle
2 Tbsp (30 mL) finely diced chives or parsley stems

One of my best recipes featuring truffles is a steamy truffle soup. The fresh truffles should be shaved over the hot soup to preserve their delicate aroma. Never overcook a truffle! Two types of truffles native to the Pacific Northwest are the Oregon black truffle and the Oregon white truffle. They are not easy to find. You would need to have a trained truffle dog or be very lucky. Truffles grow in the earth, well hidden from hungry humans. However, they give off animal pheromones to attract critters to dig them up, eat them, and distribute truffle spores throughout the forest. In the Pacific Northwest, northern flying squirrels cache them in holes in the forest as winter food, so keep an eye out for chubby-looking squirrels, though they may be hard to spot as they are nocturnal. Flying squirrels are a keystone species that relies heavily on eating truffles to survive, so I like to purchase cultivated truffles which are wicked tasty.

Place about 2 inches (5 cm) of water in a wide nonstick pan, add the vinegar and bring to a boil to poach 6 of the eggs. For foolproof pretty poached eggs crack 3 of the eggs into a fine sieve to drain off the more watery egg white and then put them gently into a small bowl. Crack the other 3 and place them in another bowl. Add each bowl of eggs to opposite sides of the boiling water in the pan. Remove with a slotted spoon after 3–4 minutes for soft poached (recommended for this recipe) and place on a plate.

Bring the stock to a boil, then turn down the heat to medium to bring it to a simmer, add the cooked rice, and cook for 20 minutes. In a medium bowl, whisk together the remaining 3 eggs and the lemon juice. Very slowly, whisk 1 cup (250 mL) of hot broth into the eggs. Reduce the heat to medium-low on the stove.

(*continued on page 197*)

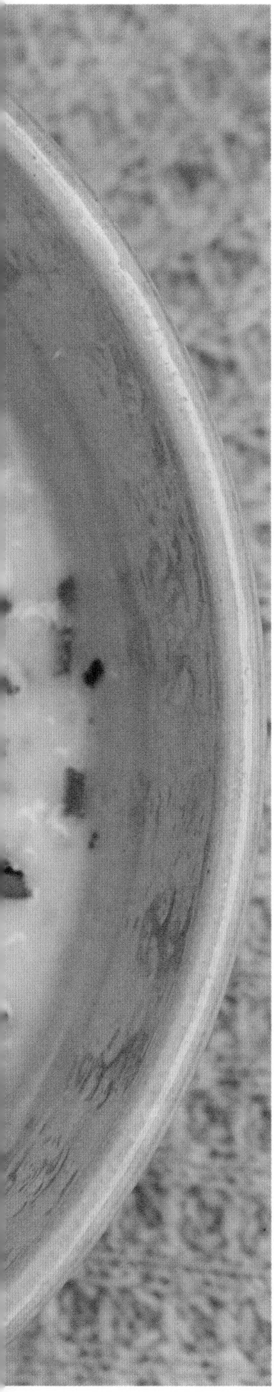

Slowly add the egg mixture to the broth, whisking constantly with a wooden spoon until thickened. It will change from transparent to more opaque when it's ready. You can also check the consistency by swiping your finger down the spoon. When it's done, it should be similar in texture to half-and-half cream. Be careful not to overcook it as it will curdle. The broth will thicken further as it cools. Turn off the heat and season to taste with salt and pepper.

Meanwhile, toast the bread to make crostini. Put the warm crostini on a side plate, drizzle with olive oil, and sprinkle with cracked salt. Pour the soup into bowls, add the poached egg, and thinly grate the truffle overtop. Use a truffle slicer to get the thinnest slices possible. Barring that, use a microplane or cheese grater. Garnish with the chives and serve hot to enjoy that gorgeous truffle aroma.

› If possible, make your own stock for this recipe. You'll definitely taste the difference.

› If you can't find truffles, buy the smallest bottle of white truffle oil you find and add about 5 drops to each bowl.

TRUFFLE HONEY MACAROONS (GF)

Makes 24 cookies

MACAROONS

1 cup (250 mL) whole hazelnuts
4 cups (1 L) unsweetened shredded coconut
6 large egg whites
Pinch of mandarin zest
½ cup (125 mL) sugar
½ tsp (2.5 mL) salt
½ tsp (2.5 mL) vanilla extract

TRUFFLE HONEY

½ cup (125 mL) liquid honey
½ tsp (2 mL) good white truffle oil
Cracked salt

The first time I tried a strong-scented white Alba truffle I was in Barcelona, Spain, at a restaurant called Cinq Sentis. The ritual of the server weighing the truffle tableside and then shaving it over your dish until you said stop was so precious. The almost salty savory richness that truffles add to a simple dish of poached egg nestled atop creamy potatoes was transportive. Ever since that moment, I have understood that fewer ingredients is better when cooking with truffles. You want to taste the truffle, uncomplicated by competing flavors, especially with an Oregon white truffle, which is more subtle than an Alba.

All truffles do well on simple recipes like these cookies, soup, handmade pasta, egg dishes, or on top of grilled meats. I think of a simple base recipe that's served hot and then about how to vary the dish in texture; a smooth sauce, chewy al dente noodles, a crunchy crouton, and finally the thinly sliced truffles with their powerful umami aroma. It's all about the scent of the truffle, so the fresher the truffle the more aroma. You must cook with it the day you get it. Each species of truffle has a different aroma profile and inherent strength—have fun!

(continued on page 200)

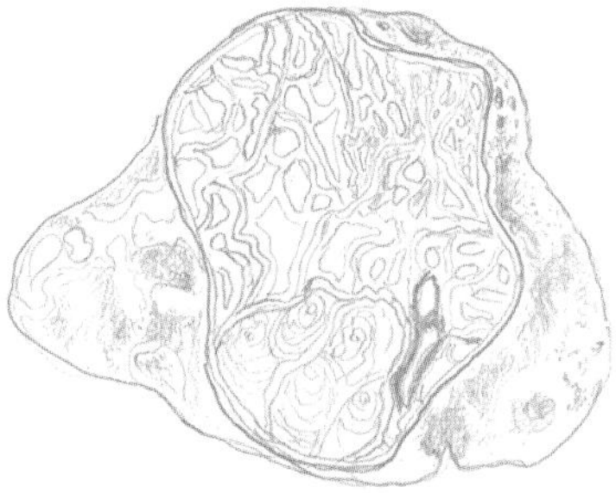

MACAROONS

Pulse the hazelnuts in a food processor fitted with the steel blade to a fine crumble. Add the coconut and process until fine, one to two pulses. Transfer to a bowl.

Place the egg whites, mandarin zest, sugar, salt, and vanilla in the food processor (no need to wipe out the bowl), and mix for about 15 seconds until light and foamy. Stir this egg mixture into the bowl with the coconut. Cover the bowl in plastic wrap and refrigerate for 30 minutes and up to 8 hours.

Place the oven racks in the upper-middle and lower-middle positions and preheat the oven to 375°F. Line two large baking sheets with greased parchment paper.

Using wet hands, roll the mixture into 1-Tbsp (15 mL) balls and lay them on the prepared baking sheets, spaced about 1 inch (2.5 cm) apart. Bake until light golden brown, 13–15 minutes. Let the macaroons cool completely on the baking sheets, about 1 hour.

TRUFFLE HONEY

Once the macaroons are completely cool, heat the honey in a saucepan on medium heat. If it's too thick, thin it with 1–3 tsp (5–15 mL) of water. You want a good pourable consistency. A pastry chef technique is to test the syrup by spooning a small drop onto a cold metal or marble surface, leave it to cool, and then test it to make sure it is thick enough to stick to the cookies slightly and yet keep them moist in texture. Turn off the heat and mix in the truffle oil. Drizzle the syrup over the cooled macaroons, sprinkle with cracked salt, and serve right away.

Seasonal foraging charts

PLANTS & MUSHROOMS

When to harvest depends on where you are and what the weather is doing. Seasons can start earlier for mushrooms the farther north or up in elevation you go. There is also variation depending on how far you are inland and what micro-climate surrounds you. Rain is a fungal friend, so when it starts to sprinkle, generally the hunt is on. When the snow comes, the mushrooms disappear. Most mushrooms love fall, but a few like to poke up in spring too. These rough charts are best for the southern British Columbia and northern Washington coastal regions. Adjust the timing back or forth depending on where you are in relation to that axis. Some places, like Oregon, have extra-long seasons that start earlier and end later than farther north where winters start earlier. Location, location, location.

Plants	Jan	Feb	Mar	Apr	May	June	July	Aug	Sept	Oct	Nov	Dec
Bittercress												
Blackberry												
Blackcap raspberry												
Cattail shoot												
Chickweed												
Conifer tips												
Dandelion flower												
Dandelion green												
Dandelion root												
Elderflower												
Fiddleheads												
Flower currant												
Huckleberries, black												
Huckleberries, red												
Juniper berry	(cones take a few years to ripen)											
Lavender												
Licorice fern												
Maple blossom												
Miner's lettuce												
Nettles							Second harvest if cut back					
Oregon grape												
Oso berry												
Purslane												
Rosehip												
Salal berry												
Salmonberry												
Saskatoon berry												
Sea asparagus												
Thimbleberry												

MUSHROOMS	April	May	June	July	Aug	Sept	Oct	Nov
Bearstooth								
Boletes	Spring King				King Bolete			
Cauliflower								
Chanterelle								
Fat Jacks								
The Gypsy								
Hawks Wing								
Hedgehog								
Honey								
Lobster								
Matsutake								
Morel								
Oyster								
The Prince								
Puffball								
Saffron Milk Caps								
Shaggy Mane								
Shrimp Russula								
White Chanterelle								
Yellowfoot Chanterelle								

SEASONAL BEACH FORAGING CHART

Harvesting shellfish in cold months is best as crabs are fattest, clams and mussels are finished reproducing so they taste better, and the water is less muddy from river outflow. However, shellfish can be eaten throughout the year in some areas along the Pacific coast. You must be very aware of water quality before harvesting any bivalve shellfish as eating bad shellfish can lead to a case of paralytic shellfish poisoning which can be fatal. Check your local government organization's website for water quality and any red tide warnings.

Seafood	Apr	May	June	July	Aug	Sept	Oct	Nov	Dec	Jan	Feb	Mar
FISH												
Crayfish (creeks)												
Surf smelt												
SEAWEEDS												
Bull kelp												
Popweed		Best in spring										
Sea lettuce												
SHELLFISH												
Clams										Best in cold months		
Crab										Best in cold months		
Mussels										Best in cold months		
Shrimp/prawn												

How to harvest seaweed

1. Make sure the water quality is top notch. Don't harvest seaweed near marinas or urban centers. The farther away from humans the better.

2. Generally, it's best to harvest seaweed when the water is cold and clear. In the summer the water can get muddy with river outflows and the flavor of the seaweed can suffer. It's still fine to pick some species in summer, but the more you harvest in areas with colder water the better the flavor will be. Some seaweeds, like bullwhip kelp, are annuals, so you can't find them in winter. Others, like popweed, can be harvested throughout the year.

3. Harvest seaweed floating on the sea surface as a sustainable best practice. These are still alive and good for harvesting as long as they look fresh and healthy. The lower the tide the more species of seaweed you will be able to access.

4. Harvest only a small amount. Seaweed is home to a lot of other creatures that rely on it for food or for breeding grounds. Don't take more than your share.

5. Not all seaweeds are edible. For example, acid kelps, which have little pouches of acid on their blades to discourage herbivores. Always identify each kelp before harvesting.

EASY-TO-IDENTIFY EDIBLE SEAWEEDS

Sea lettuce (*Ulva lactuca*): These bright green sheets of seaweed grow plentifully either attached to the rocky shoreline or once detached, in large floating colonies which are great to harvest quantities from. A very clean-tasting seaweed, great in seaweed salad and in ramen, congee, or risotto as a colorful note.

Bull kelp (*Nereocystis luetkeana*): Very easy to identify because of its large ball-shaped float and a hollow stem that can reach up to 60 inches (20 meters). Many long blades or flat leaf-like structures grow from the float up to 3 m long. Bullwhip is an annual that grows quickly in summer at about 1 foot (30 cm) a day.

Popweed (*Fucus gardneri/Fucus distictus*): Olive brown and grows to 16–20 inches (40–50 cm) long. Its flattened blades are somewhat irregularly branched. This kelp is attached, generally to rock, by a holdfast. Mature rockweed have sacks at the blade ends filled with an aloe vera–type substance.

Foraged ingredient substitutions

If you miss your window to harvest an ingredient, here is a handy chart of some store-bought alternates. Note that sometimes there isn't a viable substitute.

WILD	IN STORE
Black huckleberries	Blueberries
Bullwhip kelp blade	Nori
Burdock root	Parsnip or carrot
Chanterelle	Shiitake
Dandelion greens	Radicchio
Elderflowers	Rose petals (fresh)
Evergreen/conifer tips	Rosemary
Juniper	Cloves
Lemon balm	Fresh Oregano
Miner's lettuce	Arugula
Mugolio	Maple syrup
Nettle	Spinach
Pineapple weed	Chamomile
Plantain/Wild Greens	Watercress, arugula
Porcini	Portabello
Prince mushroom	Portabello
Sea asparagus	Asparagus
Sea lettuce	Wakame
Sugar kelp	Kombu
Surf smelt	Small trout fillet or any fresh small whitefish
Thimbleberry	Raspberry
Truffle, fresh	Truffle oil

Resources

SWALLOW TAIL COURSES

I've learned so much from so many different people throughout the years. My best advice is to find a local expert and go out on a field trip with them. My company, Swallow Tail Culinary Adventures, offers online and field trip foraging courses from sea foraging to mushroom hunting, for the Pacific Northwest region. Check our website for details on upcoming workshops in Vancouver or on the Gulf Islands. If you are in another region, feel free to contact me to see if I can help you find a teacher in your area. Here are some of my online courses so that even if you don't live near Vancouver, I can help guide you in your foraging journey.

- Virtual Foraging Survival Course
- Medicinal Plants with Métis Herbalist Lori Snyder
- Mushroom Foraging Intensive Course
- Foraging for Beginners Course
- Spring Foraging & More

A COASTAL FORAGER'S POCKET GUIDE

Check out my handy illustrated pocket guide to foraging on the Pacific Northwest coast. This brochure introduces novice foragers to 36 edible species found along our shorelines. Learn to identify, harvest, and simply prepare seaweeds, clams, sea urchins, crabs, mussels, oysters, barnacles, and more. I provide quick tips for navigating the intertidal zone that will soon have you exploring sand, rock, and wave for tasty, local, sustainable treats to add to your table. Available through retailers and via my website, swallowtail.ca.

REFERENCE BOOKS

David Arora, *Mushrooms Demystified* (1986)
Beverley Gray, *The Boreal Herbal* (2013)
Andrew MacKinnon and Linda Kershaw, *Edible and Medicinal Plants of Canada* (2016)
Amanda Swinimer, *The Science and Spirit of Seaweed* (2022)

TIPS ON HOW TO IDENTIFY WILD EDIBLES

Please refer to reputable sources for the region you are considering harvesting from and make sure that you are aware of your local harvesting regulations. If you are in the Pacific Northwest, check out Swallow Tail's online foraging programs for fungi, plants, or seafoods, or come out on a field trip with us. Visit swallowtail.ca for more info.

IDENTIFICATION TECHNIQUES

Know what you are eating! Correctly identifying a species of interest requires that you look carefully at all of its characteristics. For a plant, those features may include the root, stem, leaf, seed, fruit, and flower. Identifying a mushroom may mean looking at a spore print or how it bruises when cut, among the rest of its distinctive features. Going back to a species of interest over a full season is the best way to make sure that you are fully familiar with all its identifying characteristics throughout its growth cycle. Specimens should be typical and healthy to ensure a positive identification. Make sure that the location you find the specimen in matches its typical habitat description. Environmental factors like weather, water quality, and soil can greatly alter the shape, color, and other characteristics of any species.

LET'S KEEP IN TOUCH . . .

I'd love to hear from you and find out what you're foraging for or experimenting with in the kitchen. If you want to follow what I'm harvesting at the moment, I'm on YouTube @Swallow Tail Culinary Adventures or on Instagram @swallowtailtours or on TikTok @swallowtailculinary.

GRATITUDE

I want to thank each person who has helped make this foraging cookbook possible. First, for the centuries of knowledge gathered and shared by Indigenous coastal peoples like the Coast Salish; their expertise working with native flora and fauna helped form the backbone of my cooking with these coastal ingredients. Over the years, I've relied on experts like Andy MacKinnon and Terry Taylor to help with biological and mycological research. Thanks to Nancy Turner for her life work in documenting plant use in the Pacific Northwest and for making time to answer all my questions on whether specific plants were edible and if so how they would be eaten. Lori Snyder walked with me in her beautiful native plant garden and shared her traditional and invasive plant knowledge with me. Amanda Swinimer was ever patient helping me with all things kelp, including identification and harvesting information. Biologist and commercial crab fisherman Ficus Chan has been an instrumental partner in creating educational foraging programs at Swallow Tail and teaching me about the sea. Thank you to the talented Angela Fama for fine-tuning my food photography skills and taking some lovely photos for the book. Artist Heidi Sidhu did all the marvelous drawings for this cookbook. Jimmy Allen was invaluable in editing the first draft of my writing into the shiny penny that it is now. Thank you, all, for working with me on this heartfelt food project.

Index

NOTES

NOTES

NOTES

NOTES

NOTES

NOTES

NOTES

NOTES